Daddy, Hold Me

A Message of Hope for the Hurting

Drew Steven Becker

Copyright © 2017 Drew Steven Becker
All rights reserved.

Most Biblical citations are taken from the ESV, unless otherwise noted.
ISBN: 0692823069
ISBN 13: 9780692823064

Table of Contents

Introduction — vii

1. God Is Love — 1
2. The Colorful Expressions of a Loving Father — 10
3. Identity Affects Destiny — 23
4. He Will Free You and Fill You! — 36
5. My Steps in Healing — 44
6. Listen to What You Are Saying — 52
7. Prophesying into Your Future — 60
8. Desire the Gifts — 67
9. Love Gifts from God — 76
10. A Shout out for the Local Church — 82
11. The Rising Tide of God's Leaders — 90
12. Don't Give Up! — 102
13. Who's Chasing Who? — 110

Dedication

To My wife Christi, who is the greatest wife on the planet. Thank you for never giving up and fighting the good fight of faith with me. Nehemiah, you will stand strong and bring strength wherever you go. Ezekiel, you will bring comfort to those who need comfort. Faith, you will bring joy and deliverance to the nations. Mercy, you will be the fire of His desire.

Introduction

MY CHILDREN WANT me to pray with them every night. Sometimes they fight over me. What a great feeling: my kids love me! That does my heart good when my children want me to cuddle up to them and pray for them. Our Heavenly Father is the same. He wants our affection and voluntary love every day.

My oldest daughter, Faith, is a sweet brown-haired girl with chocolate eyes. She is our peacemaker in the family; every family needs at least one. One night I was lying in bed with my eight-year-old daughter. When I thought she was sleeping I began to lift myself out of the bed to leave her room, until she whispered, "Daddy, hold me." Wow! I felt something special about the way her gentle heart made that request. As I held my eight-year-old daughter that night, my mind was flooded with thoughts about our relationship with Father God.

Everyone on this planet is looking for validation from someone. I believe deep down inside, each of us wants that impartation of love and security that comes from our Heavenly Father. Each of us is crying deep within, "Daddy, hold me."

God is love. Our foundation as Believers in Christ is the love of God. Without this deep revelation we are constantly searching for security, validation, identity, and comfort that comes from knowing He loves me.

1
God Is Love

"Anyone who does not love does not know God, because God is love"

(1 John 4:8).

"There is no fear in love, but perfect love casts out fear. For fear has to do with punishment, and whoever fears has not been perfected in love"

(1 John 4:18).

I ASKED MY youngest daughter, Mercy, "Why do you want me to lie with you every night?" Her response was, "You make me feel safe and cozy." Safe and Cozy. The love of God is safe and cozy to those who have been broken and bruised in life.

As a young Believer in Christ, I went through a dark valley in which tears, emotional pain, and confusion seemed to be the norm for a season in my life. I clung to the promises of God and ate His Heavenly portion for my life.

> And He humbled you and let you hunger and fed you with manna, which you did not know, nor did your fathers know, that He might make you know that man does not live by bread alone, but man lives by every word that comes from the mouth of the LORD.
>
> (Deuteronomy 8:3)

When God humbles you, it's for your own good. Our Father doesn't humble us to shame us or make us a public spectacle; His humbling is for the purposes of growth, fruitfulness, and productivity. Humility activates hunger, which in turn causes you to eat from God's mouth rather than the stale bread you have been living on for far too long. I was living on stale bread, and my Daddy had more in mind for me.

I came to Christ in 1988 lying prostrate on the floor of my dorm room at Moorhead State University in Minnesota. During the previous three years, I had lived a secret double life that probably wasn't too secret to most. My heart was searching for approval and acceptance from the crowd around me, which led me to become an "approval addict" who succumbed to any temptation that would keep me part of the "Cool Tribe." Oh, how foolish.

This search for significance drove me to choose a life of lust and drinking alcohol; the two don't mix real well. Alone they can be disastrous, but like most any other demon on your back, they come in twos. I was tormented throughout high school. The pressure between knowing what's right and choosing wrong left me feeling empty and trapped.

The problem wasn't God. It was me. I had become religious, rigid, depressed, and oppressed in so many ways. It's amazing how we can experience the love and forgiveness of God that causes us to apprehend the grace of God, and then shortly thereafter, attempt to live out our walk with Christ from a rules-based mentality.

Sin is fun for a season. Moses was a mighty man of God who "chose to remain in affliction with the people of God and not to enjoy sin for a short time" (Hebrews 11:25). Not me. I chose the easy path. The path many walk because of their fear of rejection and loneliness. The Bible calls it the "fear of man": "The fear of man lays a snare, but whoever trusts in the LORD is safe" (Proverbs 29:25). A snare is a trap for catching animals. We become like a caged animal when we revere man more than we revere God.

You see, the outward actions of a person are a direct result of what's buried deep within the heart. Christianity is not about making sure you play by the rules. At the young age of twenty-one, I was "playing by all the rules," but I was miserable, suicidal, and depressed. But I was a "good boy." I was a good, religious boy full of pretense and pain. Inner pain is a tricky thing. We try to hide the pain because we know as Christians we should never have it (ha-ha-ha), and with that in mind, we strive to act better because we most certainly cannot be honest about how we are really feeling (please notice the sarcasm). That's what pretense is all about—"trying to make something that is not the case appear true" (Online Dictionary). You know how the game goes: someone asks, "How are you doing?" and your response is "Great! It couldn't be better." Liar, liar.

We choose a life that is not authentic because we are afraid God will punish us for our raw emotions that betray us when we are not able to be the "good old boy." In my pain I was forced to recognize the root cause rather than push it back down. We suppress our emotions because we say to ourselves, "We shouldn't feel that way." We serve a Big Daddy who can handle our raw emotions. He is not afraid of us; we are afraid of Him. Why? Because we truly don't understand the grace and love of God.

Who is God? God is love. What does this perfect love accomplish in our lives? It chases out fear. We are to revere God but not fear Him in the sense of being dishonest about what is really going on inside of us because we fear His punishment. He knows, He cares, and He wants us to be honest with our pain. David advised his listeners, "O my people, trust in him at all times. Pour out your heart to him, for God is our refuge" (Psalm 62:8). David was able to reveal and release his emotions unto God because he trusted Him as his refuge. A refuge is a place of safety and protection. When our view of God is not distorted, we will see Him as a place of safety and protection rather than of pain and rejection.

My first real experience with being one-hundred-percent honest and transparent was with a good friend, Mark Elhardt. Mark had just been through a journey himself that allowed him to become totally honest before the Lord. His transparency shocked me; then it became an invitation to become free. When things are left in the dark long enough, they become moldy and stale. Others may think "all is well" with us, but in reality we are becoming stale and moldy in our relationship with God because deep inside we are fearful of how He will react to our honesty.

The good news is you are not alone. Everyone who pursues the Living-Loving Father comes to this conclusion: *He can handle my pain and love me through the ugliest stuff known to humanity.* Your junk is His opportunity to show you how much He really cares and loves you. He doesn't pull you out of the muck and mire without cleaning you up. He begins a good work and completes it (Philippians 1:6).

Trials are an invitation from God to draw closer to Him. While facing trials we often focus on the pain. When we turn our eyes upon Jesus, the Author and Finisher of our faith, our faith will rise to new levels.

My journey through pain felt like the most impassable highway through the mountains of Montana, Idaho, and Washington. Two years in a row, for Christmas, our family drove from Aberdeen, South Dakota, to Seattle, Washington. Why we didn't fly, I don't know. I guess it was about bonding. The mountains were filling up with snow and the roads were becoming almost impossible to drive on. We observed accidents and an engine lying on the side of the road. Bonding alright!

After years of stuffing my pain, facing it was like driving through those snow-filled mountains. There was a strong feeling of fear and the thought, "I hope we make it!" Facing your fears and being honest about what is really happening inside of you is a lifelong journey that requires your full attention. At times it is like driving down the smooth flat highways of South Dakota—a breeze.

Why do we stuff pain? I think it's different for all of us yet generally the same. The differences are because we all have our own set of experiences, personality, emotions, and family behaviors. The similarities are the feelings of shame, guilt, fear, and remorse. Feelings are indicators of what's going on inside of us. They can be used to locate roots of pain. We have been told by well-meaning Believers in Christ, "You shouldn't feel that way, you have Christ in you the hope of glory" or "You can never trust your emotions." Listen, feelings can be indicators of pain or lies we believe.

When truth is delivered through messengers that have never faced the reality of the pain in their own heart, that truth will serve condemnation rather than transformation.

I agree. Some emotions should never lead us. We are to be led by the Spirit and not our emotions, but let's be careful about how we communicate this. For instance, when the Holy Spirit moves upon you, emotions will be expressed through crying, weeping, laughing, and shouts of joy and adoration. Those are great emotional expressions that should not be subdued. Besides, we don't serve a God that is dumb and mute like carved idols. We serve a loving Father who is colorful in expression.

Truth

God's Love

"But you, O Lord, are a God merciful and gracious, slow to anger and abounding in steadfast love and faithfulness."

(Psalm 86:15)

"The Lord is merciful and gracious, slow to anger and abounding in steadfast love."

(Psalm 103:8)

"The steadfast love of the Lord never ceases;his mercies never come to an end; 23 they are new every morning; great is your faithfulness."

(Lamentations 3:22-23)

"The LORD your God is in your midst, a mighty one who will save; he will rejoice over you with gladness; he will quiet you by his love; he will exult over you with loud singing."

(Zephaniah 3:17)

"For God so loved the world, that he gave his only Son, that whoever believes in him should not perish but have eternal life."

(John 3:16)

"But God shows his love for us in that while we were still sinners, Christ died for us."

(Romans 5:8)

"I have been crucified with Christ. It is no longer I who live, but Christ who lives in me. And the life I now live in the flesh I live by faith in the Son of God. who loved me and gave himself for me."

(Galatians 2:20)

"Beloved, let us love one another, for love is from God, and whoever loves has been born of God and knows God. Anyone who does not love does not know God, because God is love."

(1 John 4:7-8)

"We love because he first loved us."

(1 John 4:19)

Think about it...

1. What is God's purpose for humbling us?

2. Are all emotions bad?

3. Are you able to express your emotions in a healthy way?

4. Why do people suppress their pain?

2
The Colorful Expressions of a Loving Father

"The LORD is good, a stronghold in the day of trouble; he knows those who take refuge in him"

(Nahum 1:7).

"There is none like You, O LORD; You are great, and great is Your name in might"

(Jeremiah 10:6).

DEFILED RELIGION WILL always attempt to make our experience with God as drab and boring as possible. The color gray comes to mind when discussing dead religion. The Creator is colorful. I live in the great state of South Dakota. Our landscape may be flat, but our sunrises and sunsets are nothing short of breathtaking at times: the bright and brilliant orange sun with hues of yellow and gold dancing in the sky and the water reflecting the beauty of the sky.

That's what we are called to be, a reflection of His beauty. When our color reflects gray day after day, something is wrong. My reflection of the Father was gray for a long time. Something needed to change, and it wasn't my Father. It was me. Why have so many believed the lie that the more serious and downcast I am, the more holy I must be? "I'm just carrying this burden for the Lord to see His Kingdom come and His will be done. It's heavy man, heavy." That's the problem, we carry a load we were never asked to carry. We become victims of our own fleshly thinking. Last time I checked, we are called to be victors and not victims.

Our Father's Word releases us from the false obligations of carrying a heavy load: "Cast your burden on the LORD, and He will sustain you; He will never permit the righteous to be moved" (Psalm 55:22). The Hebrew word for cast is *shalak;* shalak means to throw, hurl, or fling (*Strong's Concordance*). In other words, don't be passive about ridding yourself of burdens. Don't carry around the weight of something that is contrary to the Kingdom. "For the kingdom of God is not meat and drink, but righteousness, and peace, and joy in the Holy Ghost" (Romans 14:17). Did you hear that? The Kingdom of God is not gray. The Kingdom of our Father is peace, joy, and righteousness. Full of color!

On May 1, 1991, I woke up in the morning with thoughts I had never entertained. These thoughts were from hell, yet they found a landing spot on my brain. Thoughts of killing myself flooded my mind. I remember telling someone just a few months prior to this, "I don't know why anyone has thoughts of suicide. That's crazy." Well on that first day of May, the tormenting thoughts of suicide began.

I quickly rebuked them in Jesus's name. Over and over I rebuked them. All of May I rebuked them. I found myself rebuking until my rebuker got tired—you know what I mean? I came to a conclusion quickly. I knew these thoughts weren't from God, but something had to be wrong with me internally. I'm glad I came to that conclusion. It wasn't easy but necessary for healing and restoration to manifest.

Many well-meaning Believers in Christ stumble over this. They believe it's not "faith" if we confess our weaknesses. I am all for the faith message, but when the faith message does not allow you to be transparent and honest about the afflictions, you begin to live a life filled with pretense. You have the appearance that "all is good," but deep within you know the condition of your soul (mind, will, and emotions). Your feelings are indicators that something may need healing.

God's Word prescribes steps to healing when struggling with sin: "Therefore, confess your sins to one another and pray for one another, that you may be healed. The prayer of a righteous person has great power as it is working" (James 5:16). I believe the same is true when wrestling with certain thoughts. If you make confession of them to a loving, caring person, what was once in darkness comes to the light and is exposed for what it really is—a lie.

When I opened the valve of my heart to my friend Mark in 1990, the pain of those oppressing thoughts was washed away with a rain of understanding. Why be bound when you can be freed? I became free from the lies through simply being honest about what I was thinking and feeling. How does this work? Simple. You share with another human being how you really feel and that person extends love, forgiveness, and most of all, understanding of the battle that rages in your mind. "You mean I'm not the only one who struggles with these thoughts and temptations?" That's what most people say when they enter the 101 Class of Transparency.

To lie to your brothers and sisters in Christ is self-deception. Read and listen to the following verse: "What this adds up to, then, is this: no more lies, no more pretense. Tell your neighbor the truth. In Christ's body we're all connected to each other, after all. When you lie to others, you end up lying to yourself" (Ephesians 4:25, *The Message Bible*) We can deceive ourselves by lying to others. Why choose deception rather than the truth? Because so many have found it safer lying than telling the truth. If everything is "going great," we never have to change. We would rather stay in our stronghold of lies and deception than face the truth about our condition.

This healing can come through the reading and meditating of God's Word. When I struggled intensely with depression and suicidal thoughts, God's Word became a very close and dear friend. His Word became "a lamp to my feet and a light to my path" (Psalm 119:105). The lamp brought light to my present and the light of His Word brought hope for the future.

The right kind of meditation is key for healing. Your loving Father knows the words you need right now for your healing. "My son, be attentive to my words; incline your ear to my sayings. Let them not escape from your sight; keep them within your heart. For they are life to those who find them, and healing to all their flesh" (Proverbs 4:20–22). Meditating on God's Word is the key. When I began to meditate on Scriptures like Philippians 1:6— "And I am sure of this, that He who began a good work in you will bring it to completion at the day of Jesus Christ"—hope began to fill my heart.

The mind is your greatest battlefield. What troubles the mind will trouble the emotions and eventually, if not corrected, will direct your actions. You can break addictive patterns of thinking by not just rebuking the thoughts but by replacing the lies with the truth. Jesus said to the Jewish Believers, "If you abide in my Word, you are truly my disciples, and you will know the truth, and the truth will set you free" (John 8:31–32). "We know Jesus is The Way, The Truth and The

Life, and the words He speaks are spirit and life" (John 6:63). When we abide in Jesus and eat of His Words, transformation will begin from the inside out.

The picture of the caterpillar metamorphosing into the butterfly inside the cocoon is a great picture of your transformation through living and abiding by Jesus's words. We are called out of darkness into this marvelous light to become transformed by the renewing of our minds (1 Peter 2:9; Romans 12:2).

When the mind becomes renewed, the emotions will begin to line up with what you are thinking. Meditations and musings will change from death to life, and therefore your emotions will no longer project the hurt that abides in your heart but the truth of God's Word and the life of Christ.

Remember, the Kingdom of God is righteousness, peace, and joy in the Holy Ghost (Romans 14:17). The Kingdom of God is not depression, oppression, confusion, and frustration. I was not experiencing the manifestation of my Father's Kingdom. I was experiencing the kingdom of darkness every day for nine months. The unfortunate thing is, many Believers live under a cloud for so long that they begin to adapt and cope with "their lot in life." The actual word for burden in Hebrew means *lot*, or that which is given. Sometimes that which is given is not given by your loving Father; this is necessary to discover and discern in order to perceive a true colorful reflection of Him.

Paul wrote to Timothy, "Fight the good fight of the faith" (1 Timothy 6:12). You have to fight the good fight of faith so you don't succumb to the kingdom of darkness and his lies. My life changed when I made the bold decision not to live merely by the lies that were attempting to nest on my head. I believe it was Martin Luther who said, "You can't stop the birds from flying over your head, but you can keep them from building a nest in your hair." I began to refuse the lies and declare the truth about my new identity in Christ.

Strongholds don't leave easily. You must continually resist the temptation to believe in what you have honored as truth for so long. We often honor lies above the truth. The lie has become so dear to us that we've mistakenly embraced our enemy that oppresses rather than embraced the truth that liberates. When I held the lie up to the truth, I began to hunger and thirst for what Christ purchased on the Cross for me when He said, "It is finished." Jesus said, "I have come to give you life and life more abundantly" (John 10:10). I was not experiencing the abundant life Christ provided, therefore, I went on a quest for Freedom.

Along this journey from bondage to freedom, my first discovery was the liberating power of being honest and transparent with Father and His children. The second discovery I had was the power of the tongue. The writer of Proverbs declared, "Death and life are in the power of the tongue, and those who love it will eat its fruits" (Proverbs 18:21). I was eating the fruit of negativity. Do you know what the fruit of negativity is? Hopelessness. The wind was blowing but my sails weren't up. Favor was upon me, but I was forsaking it because I simply honored lies more than I honored the truth.

The lies that assailed me were: "You will always be depressed, this is who you are." "You sinned terribly after you came to Christ. You're really not saved. You are lost." "Stay away from people. You will just depress them with all of your problems." "There is something seriously wrong with you. You are going crazy." "You are stupid." "You are not enough." The list goes on and on. I was plagued with halitosis of the mind. I needed transformation!

The summer of 1991 was my greatest challenge but also a great victory. I decided to go against what I felt and began to declare the truth of God's Word. I came into agreement with Father's Word and Father's Nature as I called into existence the things that do not exist (Romans 4:17). Faith doesn't deny the trials you are encompassed by, but it also doesn't accept the lies over the truth. When we simply live out our journey as Christians who live by the Doris Day Doctrine—"Que sera, sera, whatever will be, will be"—mentality, we surrender our God-given authority to the father of lies (John 8:44).

I was believing lies and speaking lies about myself all the time. Stop! Don't allow the devil to strip you from your God-given authority as sons and daughters of the Most High God. Decree a thing and it will come to pass (Job 22:28). Decree the truth!

The truth is, "He has delivered us from the domain of darkness and transferred us to the kingdom of his beloved Son" (Colossians 1:13). Our Father has delivered us through His Son Jesus. We were held captive as orphans to a liar who imprisons rather than empowers. As Believers and followers of Christ, we become the children of God who have been saved by a loving Father who empowers us through identity. This identity comes through the legal right given to us as Believers, "But to all who did receive Him, who believed in His name, He gave the right to become the children of God" (John 1:12). The Greek word for "right" is "exousia," which means: The delegated empowerment. Refers to the authority God gives to His Saints (HELPS Word Studies).

When we receive Christ, we are given the legal power and authority to become His children. We are no longer legally held captive by the lying thief who kills, steals, and destroys (John 10:10). This truth alone should have us shouting praises. We are free through our faith in Christ Jesus, and with that freedom, we possess an entirely new identity. With a new identity comes an entirely new perspective of life. Paul penned it well: "Therefore, if anyone is in Christ, he is a new creation. The old has passed away; behold, the new has come" (2 Corinthians 5:17). When Paul writes, "the new," he is speaking about an entirely new identity that our loving Father is zealous for us to embrace.

The question that comes to many is, "If I am a Son of God, why do I remain oppressed in my mind and emotions?" Good question. Jesus said, "If you continue in My word, then you are truly disciples of Mine; and you will know the truth, and the truth will make you free" (John 8:31–32, *New American Standard Bible*). The Word of God declares our new identity. If we know His Word about who we are as sons and daughters, the lies we clung to in our former life will be removed and replaced as we increase in knowledge.

Hosea announced to God's people, "My people are destroyed for lack of knowledge" (Hosea 4:6). If you were given an inheritance through a written will, wouldn't you want to read the details of that will? The same is true in Christ. "We have obtained an inheritance" (Ephesians 1:11). This will was signed by the Blood of Jesus that brings us into the royal family through faith. What has been written in Scripture is for our benefit to fully comprehend the details of our inheritance through Christ. To gain a clear understanding of this new identity, His Word must be illuminated to us as we meditate on it continually.

Meditation is a biblical principle. Joshua was commanded, "This Book of the Law shall not depart from your mouth, but you shall meditate on it day and night, so that you may be careful to do according to all that is written in it. For then you will make your way prosperous, and then you will have good success" (Joshua 1:8). The Hebrew word for "meditate" in this passage is "hagah," which means to utter, to muse, to mutter, to imagine (Strong's Concordance, Blue Letter Bible). In order for meditation to become fruitful in your life, you have to meditate on God's Word. It's not about freeing your mind and allowing just anything to captivate you.

Biblical meditation is pondering God's Word—uttering and musing over it. When you muse over God's Word, you are thinking about His Word intently and thoroughly. You literally become absorbed in the Power of God's thoughts. Isaiah wrote, "You keep him in perfect peace whose mind is stayed on You, because he trusts in You" (Isaiah 26:3). The word "stayed" gives us a picture of one leaning into another for support (*Strong's Concordance*). The key phrase is, "because he trusts in you." We meditate on God's Word because we trust Him.

We are called to be good stewards here on this Earth. Have you ever thought about being a good steward of your thought life? Your mind is a battlefield, and the one who overcomes in their thought life is the one who chooses to meditate on that which can bring success and prosperity—God's Word. Joshua had the law to meditate on, and it brought him prosperity and success. We have the entire written Word of God to meditate on—not to mention we are part of a New Covenant! We have Christ in us to confirm and agree with the Word that is written and spoken.

God's Word "is living and active, sharper than any two-edged sword, piercing to the division of soul and of spirit, of joints and of marrow, and discerning the thoughts and intentions of the heart" (Hebrews 4:12). When we meditate on His Word, the life of that word serves as a seed that goes into the soil of our soul and spirit to activate life to produce fruit. Jesus said, "I am the vine; you are the branches. Whoever abides in Me and I in him, he it is that bears much fruit, for apart from Me you can do nothing" (John 15:5). A major factor in abiding is meditating on the Words of Jesus. His Words are life. "It is the Spirit who gives life; the flesh is no help at all. The words that I have spoken to you are spirit and life" (John 6:63).

God's Word meditated on, then activated in your life, is a game changer. The moment I began to embrace the Words of Heaven over what I was feeling was the moment in which my life began to be founded on God's Word rather than on any experience I had or did not have. My faith increased along with hope. We let go of hope when we respect the evil and fearful reports over God's Holy Word.

Do you revere your circumstances more than you respect and revere God's Word? Isaiah wrote, "A humble and contrite person is the one who trembles at My Word" (Isaiah 66:2). To tremble at God's Word is to revere and respect Him more than your circumstances. When I read Philippians 1:6 in Dallas, Texas, back in 1991 and His Word energized me, hope sprung up in me to believe for a new day. Paul penned, "He who has begun a good work in you, will complete it." I read it, believed it, received it, confessed it, and decreed it, and I began to walk in it daily. His Word became my sustenance, my daily portion for life. Eat the Word!

Truth

The Lord is Good

"The LORD is good, a stronghold in the day of trouble; he knows those who take refugee in him."

(Nahum 1:7)

"I believe that I shall look upon the goodness of the Lord in the land of the living!"

-Psalm 27:13

"Taste and see that the LORD is good; blessed is the man who takes refuge in him."

(Psalm 34:8)

"For You, Lord, are good, and ready to forgive, And abundant in lovingkindness to all who call upon You."

(Psalm 86:5)

"Give thanks to the LORD, for he is good; his love endures forever."

(Psalm 107:1)

"You are good, and what you do is good; teach me your decrees."

(Psalm 119:68)

"The LORD is good to all; he has compassion on all he has made."

(Psalm 145:9)

"O give thanks to the LORD, for He is good; For His lovingkindness is everlasting."

(1 Chronicles 16:34)

"Every good and perfect gift is from above, coming down from the Father of the heavenly lights, who does not change like shifting shadows."

(James 1:17)

"For the Lord God is a sun and shield; the Lord bestows favor and honor. No good thing does he withhold from those who walk uprightly."

(Psalm 84:11)

Think about it...

1. What is confession good for?

2. What is transparency? Write your own definition.

3. How can you deceive yourself?

4. What is the right kind of meditation?

5. How can you break free from addictive patterns of thinking?

6. After you receive Christ as our Savior, what are you given?

7. How can you be a good steward of your thought life?

3
Identity Affects Destiny

"I will be a Father to you, and you will be my sons and daughters, says the Lord Almighty"

(2 Corinthians 6:18).

"The Spirit you received does not make you slaves, so that you live in fear again; rather, the Spirit you received brought about your adoption to sonship. And by him we cry, 'Abba, Father'"

(Romans 8:15).

GIDEON WAS A man hiding from his enemies. He was the perfect picture of someone growing content with a life controlled by fear rather than compelled with a passion for his destiny and life. Like so many today, Gideon believed a lie. The lie was exposed through a truth spoken by God to Him: "Gideon, you mighty man of valor" (Judges 6:12). Gideon's response: "Who are you talking to?" God calls forth destiny when we are living in the dungeon of doom. Gideon was hiding in a cave, working at a job that wasn't designed for him to fulfill. Why? He didn't know his true identity.

What is our true identity in Christ Jesus? Once again, we must respect God's Word over our opinion or anyone else's. We will live a lie if we don't embrace the truth that we are sons and daughters of the Most High God. As a son and daughter, you are the apple of His eye. When I discovered the richness of this truth, my life began to be transformed. My mind began to be washed and renewed through the power of His Word, which declares my new identity.

The first step in this process is realizing you have received a lie about yourself. Gideon was called out by God, and the abundance of his own heart declared what he believed: "I am the weakest of the weakest tribe." He was convinced his worth and identity came from his tribe rather than His Creator. The beautiful thing about becoming a son or daughter is this: no matter where you were born and who you were born from, God's new identity through the royal blood of Christ trumps earthly lineages. You no longer have to live under the influence of excuses as to why you are the way you are. Don't get me wrong; we are affected and infected by hurts, wounds, and abuses, but we don't have to accept that position now that we are in Christ and He is in us. You are a new creation.

Coming out of depression for me meant making different confessions of my new identity according to God's Word rather than according to any other word spoken to me on this Earth. Honestly, it was very difficult to receive. My heart was full of self-condemnation and pride. Somehow I felt I had to earn this place of prominence rather than receive it. My heart rejected His truth about me for so long, it took me months to fully believe I wasn't the fool mentioned in Proverbs. I was the son who was given the robe at a party for my return, as well as a ring representing authority.

Gideon began to believe his new identity and eventually walked in his destiny. All of us need approval from the Father. We need that heavenly impartation of validation that allows us to hear, "This is My Son, in Whom I am well pleased" (Matthew 3:17). If we don't receive the approval of God through His Son Jesus and the Holy Spirit, we search for it through other men and women; we become addicted to the approval of man. This leads to the fear of man, which is a trap.

I remember pacing the floor back and forth declaring God's Truth over my life. I wrote down several Scripture verses that declared my new identity in Christ and spoke them out loud until I memorized them. Eventually, the truth of God's Word became more powerful than the lies. When we embrace His truth, we embrace His authority. We have no authority of ourselves; it comes from His truth and the reality of who we are as His sons. If we believe a lie about ourselves, it affects our destiny. Gideon could have continued in the wine press, consumed by his fears and never seeing the power of God at work in him and through him.

In Numbers 13 Moses sent out twelve spies. Ten came back with a bad report and two a good one. The bad report reflected the lies they believed: "We are like grasshoppers in our own sight, therefore we are like grasshoppers in their sight." The writer of the Proverbs said, "What a man thinks in his heart so is he." It's important what you think about yourself. The men with the bad report affected the destiny of Israel in their generation. Without proper understanding of our God-given identities, our destinies may be aborted. Like the ten spies, we are in danger of sabotaging our own destinies through the lies we believe about ourselves.

Like the ten spies, we are in danger of sabotaging our own destinies through the lies we believe about ourselves.

We do an injustice to the Cross of Christ when we don't fully embrace who we are in Christ and who He is in us. "The message of the Cross is foolishness to those perishing, but unto us who are being saved, it is the power of God" (Romans 1:18). The Cross of Christ and His resurrection from the dead empowered Christ to empower us to be part of the family of our Father God. Why is the Cross a message of power for us being saved? The Cross speaks of a Divine exchange that happened through that royal blood that was shed. That exchange is about us no longer being sons and daughters of darkness and the devil but sons and daughters of light and power. The Father is serious about family. I'm not just talking about earthly families. I'm talking about the family that is eternal.

God gave us the right to become sons once we received Him: "But to all who did receive him, who believed in his name, he gave the right to become children of God" (John 1:12). This word "right" is a legal term meaning "the power of authority" (*Strong's Concordance, Blue Letter Bible*). In darkness, we were powerless, but in the light, we are empowered. The devil entices people with a promise of power, and the bait is attractive to some. This pseudo-power is then translated into bondage.

We have been given the power to be sons and daughters. This power is the legal right to be part of God's family through the precious blood of Jesus. We are no longer aliens or foreigners to God; we are part of an eternal family, which is thriving on Earth as well as it is in heaven. Let's lift up our heads and walk tall—not in arrogance or pride but in confidence and assurance that we are truly loved by the God of the Universe who we can call Father or Daddy. We have a great Dad!

Truth

ID In Christ

I am a Child of God

> "Yet to all who did receive him, to those who believed in his name, he gave the right to become children of God."
>
> (John 1:12)

I am a Friend of God

> "I no longer call you slaves, because the slave does not understand what his master is doing. But I have called you friends, because I have revealed to you everything I heard from my Father."
>
> (John 15:15)

I am no longer Condemned

> "There is therefore now no condemnation for those who are in Christ Jesus."
>
> (Romans 8:1)

I am an Heir of God

> "And if children, then heirs—heirs of God and fellow heirs with Christ, provided we suffer with him in order that we may also be glorified with him."
>
> (Romans 8:17)

I am More than a Conqueror

"No, in all these things we are more than conquerors through him who loved us."

(Rom. 8:37)

I am Accepted by God

"Accept one another, then, just as Christ accepted you, in order to bring praise to God."

(Romans 15:7)

I am the Temple of The Holy Spirit

"Or do you not know that your body is a temple of the Holy Spirit within you, whom you have from God? You are not your own."

(1 Corinthians 6:19)

I am bought with a Price

"For you were bought with a price. So glorify God in your body."

(1 Corinthians 6:20)

I am part of Christ's Body

"Now you are the body of Christ and individually members of it."

(1 Corinthians 12:27)

I am a victor in Christ

"But thanks be to God, who gives us the victory through our Lord Jesus Christ."

(1 Corinthians 15:57)

I am a recipient of all of God's promises

"For no matter how many promises God has made, they are 'Yes' in Christ. And so through him the 'Amen' is spoken by us to the glory of God."

(2 Corinthians 1:20)

I am a New Creation

"Therefore, if anyone is in Christ, he is a new creation. The old has passed away; behold, the new has come."

(2 Corinthians 5:17)

I am an Ambassador for Christ

"Therefore, we are ambassadors for Christ, God making his appeal through us. We implore you on behalf of Christ, be reconciled to God."

(2 Corinthians 5:20)

I am the righteousness of God in Christ

> "God made the one who did not know sin to be sin for us, so that in him we would become the righteousness of God."
>
> (2 Corinthians 5:21)

I am a Son Of God

> "For in Christ Jesus you are all sons of God, through faith."
>
> (Galatians 3:26)

I am a Child of Promise

> "Now you, brothers, like Isaac, are children of promise."
>
> (Galatians 4:28)

I am Free and no longer a slave

> "For freedom Christ has set us free. Stand firm, then, and do not be subject again to the yoke of slavery."
>
> (Galatians 5:1)

I am blessed with every spiritual blessing

> "Blessed is the God and Father of our Lord Jesus Christ, who has blessed us with every spiritual blessing in the heavenly realms in Christ."
>
> (Ephesians 1:3)

I am adopted by God

"He predestined us for adoption to himself as sons through Jesus Christ, according to the purpose of his will."

(Ephesians 1:5)

I am forgiven

"In him we have redemption through his blood, the forgiveness of our trespasses, according to the riches of his grace."

(Ephesians 1:7)

I am blessed with an inheritance

In him we have obtained an inheritance, having been predestined according to the purpose of him who works all things according to the counsel of his will.

(Ephesians 1:11)

I am saved by grace

"Even when we were dead in our trespasses, made us alive together with Christ—by grace you have been saved."

(Ephesians 2:5)

I am seated with God in heavenly places

"For he raised us from the dead along with Christ and seated us with him in the heavenly realms because we are united with Christ Jesus."

(Ephesians 2:6, New Living Translation)

I am His Masterpiece

"For we are God's masterpiece. He has created us anew in Christ Jesus, so we can do the good things he planned for us long ago."

(Ephesians 2:10, New Living Translation)

I am created in Christ for good works

"For we are his workmanship, created in Christ Jesus for good works, which God prepared beforehand, that we should walk in them."

(Ephesians 2:10)

I am united with Jesus

"But now you have been united with Christ Jesus. Once you were far away from God, but now you have been brought near to him through the blood of Christ."

(Ephesians 2:13, New Living Translation)

I am a member of God's Household

> "So then you are no longer strangers and aliens, but you are fellow citizens with the saints and members of the household of God."
>
> (Ephesians 2:19)

I am a home to God's power and His power is working in me

> "Now to him who is able to do far more abundantly than all that we ask or think, according to the power at work within us."
>
> (Ephesians 3:20)

I am living in The Light

> "For at one time you were darkness, but now you are light in the Lord. Walk as children of light."
>
> (Ephesians 5:8)

I am a citizen of Heaven

> "But our citizenship is in heaven, and from it we await a Savior, the Lord Jesus Christ."
>
> (Philippians 3:20)

I am holy and blameless in Christ

> "He has now reconciled in his body of flesh by his death, in order to present you holy and blameless and above reproach before him."
>
> (Colossians 1:22)

I am a chosen one

> "But you are a chosen race, a royal priesthood, a holy nation, a people for his own possession, that you may proclaim the excellencies of him who called you out of darkness into his marvelous light."
>
> (1 Peter 2:9)

I am a royal priest

> "But you are a chosen race, a royal priesthood, a holy nation, a people for his own possession, that you may proclaim the excellencies of him who called you out of darkness into his marvelous light."
>
> (1 Peter 2:9)

I am part of a holy nation

> "But you are a chosen race, a royal priesthood, a holy nation, a people for his own possession, that you may proclaim the excellencies of him who called you out of darkness into his marvelous light."
>
> (1 Peter 2:9)

Think about it...

1. Do you known your true Identity in Christ?

2. What is your perspective about yourself?

3. Are you believing God's truth or a lie about yourself?

4. What steps will you take to understand your true identity in Christ?

4
He Will Free You and Fill You!

"So if the Son sets you free, you will be free indeed"

(John 8:36).

"And do not get drunk with wine, for that is debauchery, but be filled with the Spirit"

(Ephesians 5:8).

AFTER NINE SOLID months of suffering with tormenting thoughts of suicide coupled with crushing oppression, I was about to give up. I spent hours writing, praying, and thinking, trying to figure out what was wrong with me. Hours of my life were consumed with introspection. The more I looked in, the less I looked up. When we become consumed with "What's wrong with me?" we lose our focus quickly.

Years ago I had a powerful dream. In the dream the ground began to shake and rumble. As the ground continued to move, a large object emerged, rising slowly and powerfully. It was a huge lighthouse. When it rose to its peak, arms thrust out with great force and transformed into Jesus Himself. I woke up immediately with this Scripture in my thoughts: "Looking unto Jesus, the author and finisher of our faith" (Hebrews 12:2). That dream has been forever etched in my mind.

When surrounded by various trials, our goal should not be to look within as much as to look up. Our deliverance doesn't draw near when we withdraw and become introspective. Our deliverance comes when we continue to look up. Jesus is the author and finisher of our faith. What He started He will complete, if we continue to look to Him, the author and finisher.

The Psalmist wrote, "I lift up my eyes to the hills. From where does my help come? My help comes from the LORD, who made heaven and earth" (Psalm 121:1–2). Our focus is our choice. If we choose to keep our focus on the problems and attempt to solve them with our own understanding, we will not be empowered; we will become discouraged. The Psalmist looked to the hills. Why the hills? Hills and mountains often represent revelation. Moses received revelation on Mount Sinai and radiated with the Presence of God. Revelation comes through our relationship with Father, Son, and Holy Spirit. Through relationship we receive a revelation that empowers us to overcome, so we don't become overpowered with hopelessness.

At the beginning of 1992, I had come to the end of myself. I will remember that day as long as I live. It was a Sunday afternoon shortly after the Sunday morning service. I came home with a sense of hopelessness and despair as I called a friend and said these words: "I'm so sick and tired of being sick and tired. I give up." Shortly after I said those words on the phone I heard in my spirit: "Good, now I can move." I thought to myself, "Was that God?" Yes, it was God Himself speaking to me.

When I ceased to attempt to figure everything out in my own head and strive to do everything perfectly, I began to arrive at a place called rest. You may call it a place of trust. About two weeks after that conversation on the phone, I began to discover what "Good, now I can move" meant. You can say I had a powerful encounter with God. Do you know what happens when you encounter God? You change!

The encounter happened in the sanctuary of First Assembly in Fargo, North Dakota. First Assembly was hosting meetings with Rodney Howard-Browne. The church was positioned for a move of God. People were hungry for something fresh. Pastor Dan Rothwell prepared us for something special to happen prior to Rodney coming to Fargo. I was personally desperate for a move of God in my life. Like I said before, I had come to the end of myself and needed God's intervention.

One particular evening I said to myself, "enough is enough." Rodney was walking throughout the building, laying hands on people and watching them get touched by God. He began to walk down the middle aisle in which I was sitting. Instead of hoping he would pray for me, I decided to stand up and walk towards him with a look of great desperation. He said, "What do you need?" I remember saying, "I am depressed and have thoughts of suicide." That's about all I remember when he laid hands on my head and rebuked the spirit of suicide. Immediately after I fell to the ground, screams came out of my mouth I had never heard before.

Honestly, I knew at that moment I was being delivered by the Power of God. Many people become embarrassed after such an encounter, but I didn't care anymore. I just wanted to be free. The pride had to be removed before the freedom came to my life. My parents were sitting with me that night at church. My mom said I looked like a snake as I moved along the floor. I was not possessed by the devil, but I certainly was oppressed. But "If the Son sets you free, you will be free indeed" (John 8:36). Once again, if you truly want to be free, your hunger must supersede your personal pride. You must come to the point where you don't care how it looks; you just want to come to the place of liberty.

After that encounter with God, I stood up in the sanctuary and felt different, like, "What just happened to me?" About two minutes later, Rodney prayed for me again in his English accent, saying, "Fill it up. Lord fill him." What I encountered after that was transformational. I began to laugh and cry for the next two weeks. Every thought that was used as a weapon to torment me, prior to my deliverance, was now being laughed at in the manifest presence of God. The thoughts would come, and I would laugh. It was like I laughed my way to victory. I know it sounds strange but Scripture tells us, "A joyful heart is good medicine, but a crushed spirit dries up the bones" (Proverbs 17:22). I was crushed, and God was pouring in His medicine to heal.

When I cried, it was very deep. God's way of healing the heart is through laughter and tears. I was on God's operating table. My tears reflected two things: (1) pain that was locked up in my heart and (2) gratefulness for the intense love I felt as He was healing me from all the brokenness. God is good. Never forget this truth: God is good!

The Scripture that emerged for me was from Psalm 126:1–2:

> "A Song of Ascents. When the LORD restored the fortunes of Zion, we were like those who dream. Then our mouth was filled with laughter, and our tongue with shouts of joy; then they said among the nations, "The LORD has done great things for them."

God was restoring me, and it was like a dream. My mouth was filled with laughter, and shouts of praise and adoration came out of my mouth declaring the goodness of God. I remember what the Lord shared with me after this encounter, **"Drew, I can do more in one second than you can do in a lifetime."** It's true. All the struggling and striving to be perfect came crumbling down in His Presence. At this moment in my life, the cry of my heart was, "Daddy, hold me!" And you know what? He held me, and He healed me like no other person can do on this planet.

Truth

Freedom

"If you then, who are evil, know how to give good gifts to your children, how much more will the heavenly Father give the Holy Spirit to those who ask him!"

(Luke 11:13)

"It is the Spirit who gives life; the flesh is no help at all. The words that I have spoken to you are spirit and life."

(John 6:63)

"So Jesus said to the Jews who had believed him, 'If you abide in my word, you are truly my disciples, and you will know the truth, and the truth will set you free.'"

(John 8:31-32)

"So if the Son sets you free, you will be free indeed."

(John 8:36)

"Now the Lord is the Spirit, and where the Spirit of the Lord is, there is freedom."

(2 Corinthians 3:17)

"There is therefore now no condemnation for those who are in Christ Jesus. For the law of the Spirit of life has set you free in Christ Jesus from the law of sin and death."

(Romans 8:1-2)

"That the creation itself will be set free from its bondage to corruption and obtain the freedom of the glory of the children of God."

(Romans 8:21)

"Now the Lord is the Spirit, and where the Spirit of the Lord is, there is freedom."

(2 Corinthians 3:17)

"In the same way we also, when we were children, were enslaved to the elementary principles of the world. But when the fullness of time had come, God sent forth his Son, born of woman, born under the law, 5 to redeem those who were under the law, so that we might receive adoption as sons. And because you are sons, God has sent the Spirit of his Son into our hearts, crying, 'Abba! Father!' So you are no longer a slave, but a son, and if a son, then an heir through God."

(Galatians 4:3-7)

Think about it...

1. What is the problem with becoming too introspective?

2. Are you more focused on your problems or The LORD? If you need to change your focus, how will you do it?

3. Where does revelation and insight come from?

4. Write down three ways you can focus on the positive rather than the negative?

5
My Steps in Healing

"For I am the LORD, your healer"

(Exodus 15:26b).

"For I know the plans I have for you, declares the LORD, plans for welfare and not for evil, to give you a future and a hope"

(Jeremiah 29:11).

EVERYONE WHO HAS experienced The Living-Loving Father has his or her own story to tell. Each story is about a process in which the Holy Spirit led each person through to discover the healing touch of Jesus. My journey is different than yours, but the life-giving principles found in the Bible can be applied to anyone hungry to become free.

My journey began with a discovery: I needed help! My personal pride held me captive to a life filled with pain and a denial that anything was wrong. You have heard the statement, "You are in denial." Well I was in denial and needed a reality check. I knew the right things to say and how to act but inwardly was bleeding. When I admitted to myself and others that I was broken, the process of healing could begin.

I just had a conversation with someone who hates his job. They called me to tell me how much they hate it and why. This person said they called me for help. I asked them, "How can I help?" I think they just wanted me to show them some sympathy for being at a job for several years and not making much money. You know what I told them, "Get a different job!" You see, oftentimes we invite others to our pity party because honestly, we don't want to change. We just want others to sympathize with our stupidity. God will never anoint stupidity. He will anoint a person who takes responsibility and is willing to change, but He will not show up for your pity party. I know that sounds tough, but sometimes we need tough love.

In my season of pain, I discovered the loving and gracious presence of Jesus, and I also encountered a loving Father who disciplines because He loves me. "For the Lord disciplines the one He loves, and chastises every son whom He receives" (Hebrews 12:6). In August of 1991, I went to the home of Bob and Tania Goos. I asked them to pray for me and take authority over anything that was troubling me. I shared my heart and struggles and they began to pray. I remember Tania praying against many things, but one specific thing she said struck me immediately: "We come against that pity spirit!" I thought, "pity spirit!?" I was almost offended.

I cannot remember who said it years ago—"God will offend the mind to reveal the heart"—but that's exactly what happened. My mind got offended, and it was precisely what I needed to hear. I'm not sure I would have received that message from anyone other than

Tania. Pride and pity are buddies. Pride will say, "There is nothing wrong with me," and pity will proclaim, "Look what others have done to me to make my life miserable." Both attitudes or spirits will avoid being responsible for personal actions.

Pride keeps us in bondage to a skewed view of reality. Our view becomes distorted with pride because we see the changes everyone else should make, but aren't able to see the changes we should make. Pride poisons our spirit and makes us the judge and jury. It literally robs us of becoming the loving person Jesus wants us to become. It keeps us in bondage to our own self-deception. Pride's mantra is, "I am right and you are wrong". When we are always right, we will never see the need for change.

Pride points the finger at everyone else and refuses to receive correction. In the previous chapter, I wrote about becoming too introspective. When pride is dominating a person's life, self-examination is rare.

I began to discover the depths of pride in my life through a number of experiences. In college, I would pretty much say whatever I thought. That often revealed the foolishness and pride of my heart. Scripture declares, "Even a fool who keeps silent is considered wise; when he closes his lips, he is deemed intelligent. (Proverbs 17:28). Needless to say, I was rarely accused of being wise or intelligent in my early years of college. I said what I thought and declared what I felt. President Abraham Lincoln said, "Better to remain silent and be thought a fool than to speak and to remove all doubt." I certainly didn't want to feed into anyone's doubt about my pride and ignorance.

I remember saying foolish things and hurting people's feelings. It rarely bothered me, until one particular day, a young lady approached me with my offensive ways. It's called, confrontation. She confronted me and communicated how my words hurt and offended her. The Holy Spirit used her that day to challenge me. I was challenged to look within and see the need for change.

What was the issue of my heart? Pride. It manifested through my words everyday. I had more opinions than actual solutions. Watchmen Nee once said, "An opinionated man is an unbroken man." That was me. I had opinions about everyone and everything. I was the proverbial "know it all". What I didn't know at the time was: The pride in my heart, was keeping God's Presence from flowing in me to bring health and healing.

Let's call them walls. What do walls do? They protect you. Pride protects you from the painful process of possessing the revelation of the real problem. What was the real problem in my life? I was hurt by others and extremely insecure. Rather than allowing The Presence of God to heal the hurt, I put up walls so no one could hurt me. Hurting people, hurt people as a defense mechanism. If someone is suffering from rejection, they will reject you before you can reject them. If someone is insecure, they attempt to hide the insecurity. How? It depends on the wound and the personality.

Some hide insecurity through humor. They become the "class clown" and lime-light of every party. Others crawl in a cave and become deathly afraid of people they aren't comfortable with. The opinionated ones, often hide their insecurities by feeling the need to know everything. Each type is attempting to protect their pain that Jesus wants to heal.

Let go of your pride. Become vulnerable through being completely honest and transparent about the condition of your soul. This is a choice only you can make. By choosing humility, you choose healing. Why? Because humility attracts the manifest presence of

God. King Uzziah began his reign over Judah at a very young age. He started strong. He listened to the prophet Zechariah and was obedient unto God. Later in his reign, he decided to listen to his own counsel rather than God's. He became proud.

The prophet Isaiah wrote, "In the year that King Uzziah died I saw the Lord sitting upon a throne, high and lifted up; and the train of his robe filled the temple." (Isaiah 6:1). King Uzziah was the epitome of pride. When pride dies in our life, we too will see The Lord high and lifted up. Uzziah literally means: "My strength is Jehovah" (Strongs Concordance). The moment we forget The Lord is our strength, is the moment we begin to function under the banner of pride. If you rid yourself of pride, God's Presence will increase in your life and the healing process will begin. John the Baptist summed it up well, "He must increase, but I must decrease." (John 3:30). Let's allow God to increase, and our pride decrease. It's time to heal.

Truth

Healing & Restoration

"Bless the Lord, O my soul, and forget not all his benefits, who forgives all your iniquity, who heals all your diseases, who redeems your life from the pit, who crowns you with steadfast love and mercy"

(Psalm 103:2-4)

"He heals the brokenhearted and binds up their wounds."

(Psalm 147:3)

"Heal me, O Lord, and I shall be healed; save me, and I shall be saved, for you are my praise."

(Jeremiah 17:14)

"For I will restore health to you, and your wounds I will heal, declares the Lord, because they have called you an outcast: 'It is Zion, for whom no one cares!'"

(Jeremiah 30:17)

"Behold, I will bring to it health and healing, and I will heal them and reveal to them abundance of prosperity and security."

(Jeremiah 33:6)

"And the Lord restored the fortunes of Job, when he had prayed for his friends. And the Lord gave Job twice as much as he had before."

(Job 42:10)

"And after you have suffered a little while, the God of all grace, who has called you to his eternal glory in Christ, will himself restore, confirm, strengthen, and establish you."

(1 Peter 5:10)

"Come, let us return to the Lord; for he has torn us, that he may heal us; he has struck us down, and he will bind us up."

(Hosea 6:1)

"But he gives more grace. Therefore it says, 'God opposes the proud, but gives grace to the humble.'"

(James 4:6)

"Therefore, confess your sins to one another and pray for one another, that you may be healed. The prayer of a righteous person has great power as it is working."

(James 5:16)

"Beloved, I pray that all may go well with you and that you may be in good health, as it goes well with your soul."

(3 John 1:2)

Think about it...

1. What are the signs of pride? How do you know pride is in your life?

2. How can pride prevent you from becoming whole?

3. How can you rid yourself of pride?

4. Do you desire change or pity from others? How do you know?

6
Listen to What You Are Saying

"From the same mouth come blessing and cursing. My brothers, these things ought not to be so"

(James 3:10).

"Lord, make my words as sweet as honey, for tomorrow I may have to eat them!"

—Anonymous

HAVE YOU EVER taken a moment to listen to yourself? What's coming out of your own mouth? Are your words bringing life to others or death? Do you walk in the room and stir everything up with your words, or do you bring peace? A lot of questions to ask yourself, but until you do, an honest evaluation cannot be made of the words you are speaking.

Where do our words originate? Jesus said, "For the mouth speaks what the heart is full of" (Luke 6:45, NLT). If your heart is full of hate, jealousy, anger, and bitterness, your words will not be sweet but bitter. The words you speak will be critical, harsh, cutting, and at times extremely sarcastic. If your heart is full of love, joy, and peace, you will speak words of encouragement, building and producing peace in the hearts of those listening.

The words we speak reveal a deeper truth about ourselves. If we can detect what we are saying and the attitude in which we are saying it, the desired healing can come. If you are hungry for healing, then you will be honest with yourself and judge the words you are speaking. Paul wrote, "But if we judged ourselves truly, we would not be judged" (1 Corinthians 11:31). One way we can judge ourselves is by carefully listening to the words coming out of our mouths. Remember this: The tune of your tongue reveals the tone of your heart.

The good news is, we can monitor our own heart. I didn't say *heal* our own heart, but monitor or manage it. Throughout our lives we learn to manage our money, food intake, homes, cars, jobs, and the list goes on. Your heart will be the most important thing you manage. "Above all else, guard your heart, for everything you do flows from it." (Proverbs 4:23, NIV). The Hebrew word for guard is "nastar," which means to preserve, guard from dangers, blockade, or watch (*Strong's Concordance, Blue Letter Bible*). Above everything else we are to be the guardians or watchmen over the most important thing: our heart.

What goes in will come out. You've heard the old adage, "Garbage in, garbage out." The opposite is also true, "Life in, life out." What we gaze upon we become. Our eyes and ears are highways for life or death, and we have the power to choose what travels down those roads. "Finally, brothers, whatever is true, whatever is honorable, whatever is just, whatever is pure, whatever is lovely, whatever is commendable, if there is any excellence, if there is anything worthy of praise, think about these things" (Philippians 4:8). Scripture gives us the standard of those things we are to be meditating on. When our gaze is upon the Lord and His Word, our heart will be guarded and our words will produce life.

A great prayer is, "Let the words of my mouth and the meditation of my heart be acceptable in your sight, O Lord, my rock and my redeemer" (Psalm 19:14). Once again, God and His Word is our standard. The Psalmist didn't pray, "May my words and thoughts be acceptable to my friends and the World." He prayed, "acceptable in your sight." The Lord sees and hears our words and knows our thoughts. When our quest is to please Him, we will become much better guardians of our hearts. Like the Psalmist let us declare, "I will meditate on your precepts and fix my eyes on your ways" (Psalm 119:15). Set yourself up for success by choosing to declare your path and remain fixed on it.

We are promised health and success when our meditation is upon God and His Word. "My son, be attentive to my words; incline your ear to my sayings. Let them not escape from your sight; keep them within your heart. For they are life to those who find them, and healing to all their flesh" (Proverbs 4:20–22). We inject life into our souls and healing in our flesh when we hide God's Word in our hearts. I like what the Psalmist wrote: "I have stored up your word in my heart, that I might not sin against you" (Psalm 119:11). God's Word, His Standard, is our rule of life. When we embrace His Word we embrace life. When we refuse and rebel against His Word, we embrace death.

Another promise is peace. Who doesn't want peace? God's peace in our hearts is like a well-watered garden. Without His peace, we are riddled with anxiety and fear. Peace is a byproduct of our meditation. "You keep him in perfect peace whose mind is stayed on you, because he trusts in you" (Isaiah 26:3). To be in perfect peace is to be completely at peace, a place of rest. When we keep our focus on our Author and Finisher of our faith and not our circumstances, peace will guard us from the heat of anxiety. I compare anxiety to heat because it attempts to make you weary. Peace gives strength; anxiety and worry weaken you. When anxiety rules, your perception changes dramatically.

Anxiety can be overcome through prayer and a decision to not embrace it. "Do not be anxious about anything, but in everything by prayer and supplication with thanksgiving let your requests be made known to God. And the peace of God, which surpasses all understanding, will guard your hearts and your minds in Christ Jesus" (Philippians 4:6–7). Don't be anxious! It's a command. It's also permission from Heaven not to be bound by something so earthly and demonic. Some people need to hear, "You don't have to worry. You can trust God!" When you decide not to worry, you replace it with prayer, supplication, thanksgiving, and making your requests known to God. It's not enough to stop sinning. You have to start living according to God's Word once you decide to stop worrying.

When consumed by worry, peace has no place. But when worry is renounced, it can be replaced with the peace of God that guards your heart and mind. You become a guardian of your heart and mind when you refuse to worry and replace the worry with your prayers, supplication, and thanksgiving. When we have peace we have a place where our mind can think clearly, our words become life-giving, and our actions glorify the Lord.

Anxiety produces depression (Proverbs 12:25). Depression weakens our ability to persevere through trials and overcome negative and discouraging thoughts. We can begin to remove depression by resolving in our hearts and minds to no longer meditate on the things that want to weigh us down. You may be saying right now, "It's not that easy!" I agree. It's not that easy! It takes a hungry person to make a solid commitment to becoming whole. Change requires disciplining oneself to think differently and talk differently. When you have succumbed to believing the lie, "I will never change," it's hard to change. But when you believe that transformation is possible through your relationship with Jesus, hope is on its way.

Transformation is possible through God's Word. When you become renewed in your mind, you exchange the lies that have bound you for the Truth that frees you.

"I appeal to you therefore, brothers, by the mercies of God, to present your bodies as a living sacrifice, holy and acceptable to God, which is your spiritual worship. Do not be conformed to this world, but be transformed by the renewal of your mind, that by testing you may discern what is the will of God, what is good and acceptable and perfect" (Romans 12:1–2). Transformation begins with a decision that you make to surrender your entire being to God—Father, Son, and Holy Spirit. Surrender precedes transformation. If excuses are continually made, change will not come. If you resist the Word and embrace your old and familiar ways of thinking, bondage is inevitable. Make the declaration, "I can change and I will change through meditating and confessing God's Powerful Word!" You can do it! You can change through the Power of God's Word and by His Spirit.

Truth

Words

"There is one whose rash words are like sword thrusts, but the tongue of the wise brings healing."

(Proverbs 12:18)

"Whoever guards his mouth preserves his life; he who opens wide his lips comes to ruin."

(Proverbs 13:3)

"Death and life are in the power of the tongue, and those who love it will eat its fruits."

(Proverbs 18:21)

"Let the words of my mouth and the meditation of my heart be acceptable in your sight, O Lord, my rock and my redeemer."

(Psalm 19:14)

"Set a guard, O Lord, over my mouth; keep watch over the door of my lips!"

(Psalm 141:3)

"Let no corrupting talk come out of your mouths, but only such as is good for building up, as fits the occasion, that it may give grace to those who hear."

(Ephesians 4:29)

"I tell you, on the day of judgment people will give account for every careless word they speak."

(Matthew 12:36)

"But what comes out of the mouth proceeds from the heart, and this defiles a person."

(Matthew 15:18)

"The good person out of the good treasure of his heart produces good, and the evil person out of his evil treasure produces evil, for out of the abundance of the heart his mouth speaks."

(Luke 6:45)

Think about it...

1. Are your words bringing life to others or death?

2. From where do our words originate?

3. What does the tune of your tongue reveal?

4. How can you manage your heart?

5. What is God's Word profitable for?

6. Why are you anxious?

7. Memorize: Isaiah 26:3; Philippians 4:6-8; and Romans 12:1-2.

7
Prophesying into Your Future

"And it shall come to pass afterward, that I will pour out my Spirit on all flesh; your sons and your daughters shall prophesy, your old men shall dream dreams, and your young men shall see visions"

(Joel 2:28).

"But he that prophesieth speaketh unto men to edification, and exhortation, and comfort"

(1 Corinthians 14:3, KJV).

ONE NIGHT AS I was driving around in my car in the Fargo/Moorhead area, a prophetic anointing began to flow out of my mouth. I heard others prophesy in church, but I didn't flow in the gift of prophecy much at this time in my life. Most prophetic words I heard were at large church gatherings and were loud and sometimes very powerful.

The first time I was ever prophesied over was in 1988 by a man named Moses Veigh. Moses was a big man with a booming voice and white hair—imagine that. I can remember distinctly how I felt: loved, encouraged, and challenged to go deeper in my relationship with Jesus. Sounds like a true prophetic word to me. That was twenty-seven years ago, and I can still remember the words that came out of his mouth. By the way, the words have come to pass in my life.

As I was driving, I found myself prophesying to myself. At the time it was very strange to me. I remember thinking, "Can I do this? Is this biblically correct?" I laugh at that now. If prophetic words are designed to encourage, strengthen, and comfort (1 Corinthians 14:3), why couldn't we prophesy over ourselves? If you cannot encourage yourself, how in the world are you going to encourage others? You're not!

David and his mighty men were away from their families while battling their enemies. They were on a conquest. When they returned to their homes in Ziklag, they found their homes burned to the ground and their wives and children taken captive by their enemies. At this discouraging moment, David and his men began to weep bitterly because of their great loss.

Out of intense pain from their loss, David's men began to turn against him.

> "And David was greatly distressed, for the people spoke of stoning him, because all the people were bitter in soul, each for his sons and daughters"
>
> (1 Samuel 30:6).

That's how pain works. When in the depths of despair, surely something or someone is at fault and the "blame game" begins. The six hundred men, who were extremely loyal to David and his cause, began talking about stoning him. This can be the plight of leaders; they make the tough decisions and have to navigate their team when things go horribly wrong.

When the chips are down and everyone wants your head on a platter, what do you do? Most of us would run for the hills. Not David. David's anointed leadership shines through this story. He didn't run. "But David strengthened himself in the LORD his God" (1 Samuel 30:6). David encouraged himself in the Lord. He found strength from Heaven when Earth was crying out for his blood.

David knew that times like these required him to look up rather than look within. David said to the priest, Abiathar, "Bring me the ephod" (1 Samuel 30:7). An ephod was originally worn by the High Priest and then later by ordinary priests (*Easton's Bible Dictionary*). This garment was set apart for priests (Jewish Encyclopedia) who ministered unto the Lord. Under intense pressure, David asked for the ephod to inquire of the Lord. The crossroads of life require the wisdom of the Lord. The ephod represented David's connection to the Lord, his covering and light upon his path.

David's future depended on his refusal to remain in pity and pain. Rather than dying in Ziklag, he chose to go to the Heavenly Zion, which lifted him above the temporal and into his destiny. Ziklag means winding (*Strong's Concordance*). David's path appeared to be "winding down." When David looked up, his path became straight. When we seek the Lord, He will speak to us. His perspective becomes our perspective. His Words become our words. Words that we declare! Words that make straight our paths to a Divine destiny rather than a pitiful present.

That night in Fargo/Moorhead, I called out to the Lord, and He showed me great and mighty things (Jeremiah 33:3). My words lined up with His words! My thoughts lined up with His thoughts! Zion roared and Ziklag left. No more winding down, but rising above the pain and the pity. That's what the prophetic anointing will do; it will lift you up and keep you from wallowing in your pain. That night I learned a valuable Kingdom Principle: I can encourage myself in the Lord by calling out to Him, hearing His voice, and prophesying over my future.

Truth

Prophesy

"We have different gifts, according to the grace given to each of us. If your gift is prophesying, then prophesy in accordance with your faith"

(Romans 12:6)

"Pursue love, and earnestly desire the spiritual gifts, especially that you may prophesy."

(1 Corinthians 14:1)

On the other hand, the one who prophesies speaks to people for their upbuilding and encouragement and consolation.

(1 Corinthians 14:3)

"For you can all prophesy one by one, so that all may learn and all be encouraged."

(1 Corinthians 14:31)

"Do not quench the Spirit. Do not despise prophecies."

(1 Thessalonians 5:19-20)

"And it shall come to pass afterward, that I will pour out my Spirit on all flesh; your sons and your daughters shall prophesy, your old men shall dream dreams, and your young men shall see visions. Even on the male and female servants in those days I will pour out my Spirit. 'And I will show wonders in the heavens and on the earth, blood and fire and columns of smoke. The sun shall be turned to darkness, and the moon to blood, before the great and awesome day of the Lord comes. And it shall come to pass that everyone who calls on the name of the Lord shall be saved. For in Mount Zion and in Jerusalem there shall be those who escape, as the Lord has said, and among the survivors shall be those whom the Lord calls.'"

(Joel 2:28-32)

"But this is what was uttered through the prophet Joel: 'And in the last days it shall be, God declares, that I will pour out my Spirit on all flesh, and your sons and your daughters shall prophesy, and your young men shall see visions, and your old men shall dream dreams; even on my male servants and female servants in those days I will pour out my Spirit, and they shall prophesy. And I will show wonders in the heavens above and signs on the earth below, blood, and fire, and vapor of smoke; the sun shall be turned to darkness and the moon to blood, before the day of the Lord comes, the great and magnificent day.'"

(Acts 2:16-21)

Think about it...

1. When you prophesy, three powerful things happen. List those three things.

2. What did David do when everyone wanted to kill him?

3. Why is it important to encourage yourself in the LORD?

4. How can you encourage yourself in the LORD?

5. Are you encouraged or discouraged? Why?

8
Desire the Gifts

"Now concerning spiritual gifts, brothers, I do not want you to be uninformed"

(1 Corinthians 12:1).

"So you should earnestly desire the most helpful gifts. But now let me show you a way of life that is best of all"

(1 Corinthians 12:31).

GROWING UP IN church was a huge advantage for me. I was taught basic biblical principles and experienced the power of the community of Believers. Thank God for the local church! I'm a big fan. It was the local church that taught me to believe for miracles and desire spiritual gifts.

In my earlier years of formation, we were taught to "Seek the Giver not the gifts" and "The fruit of The Spirit is more important than the gifts of The Holy Spirit." For whatever reason, we are conditioned to believe certain characteristics of God are more important than others. A more balanced view embraces both; the gifts of The Spirit and the fruit of The Spirit.

Paul's letter to the Galatians describes the nine fruits of the Spirit, "But the fruit of the Spirit is love, joy, peace, patience, kindness, goodness, faithfulness, gentleness, self-control; against such things there is no law" (Galatians 5:22-23). Obviously, it's important as a Believer in Christ to walk in The Spirit so we display the fruit of The Spirit. I would never minimize the importance of manifesting the fruits of The Spirit.

Later in my development, I discovered you can seek the Giver and the gifts, and spiritual gifts are important and should not be minimized to believing that only the "super spiritual" can flow in the gifts of the Holy Spirit. Paul writes to the Corinthians, "To each is given the manifestation of the Spirit for the common good. For to one is given through the Spirit the utterance of wisdom, and to another the utterance of knowledge according to the same Spirit, to another faith by the same Spirit, to another gifts of healing by the one Spirit, to another the working of miracles, to another prophecy, to another the ability to distinguish between spirits, to another various kinds of tongues, to another the interpretation of tongues" (1 Corinthians 12:7-10). The gifts of The Spirit are for the good of all. They are expressions God's love to people. If I want to demonstrate God's love to people, I will desire the gifts of The Holy Spirit.

Paul wrote to the Corinthians, "Now concerning spiritual gifts, I do not want you to be uninformed" (1 Corinthians 12:1). Paul didn't want God's people remaining ignorant of these powerful gifts because they are gifts from God. Why wouldn't we want everything God has for us? I'm glad you asked. Spiritual fruit is easier for us to wrap our brain around. Stay close to Jesus, become more like Jesus. But spiritual gifts? How do they work? How are they demonstrated? We attempt to understand with the mind something that can only function by His Spirit.

"The natural person does not accept the things of the Spirit of God, for they are folly to him, and he is not able to understand them because they are spiritually discerned" (1 Corinthians 2:14). Paul is not talking to the heathens. He is talking to Christians who could not be addressed as spiritual: "But I, brothers, could not address you as spiritual people, but as people of the flesh, as infants in Christ" (1 Corinthians 3:1). I'm not saying that everyone who speaks in tongues and prophesies is more spiritual. Not at all. In fact, I have seen some who speak in tongues and prophesy do some of the craziest fleshly things. How can that be?

It's possible because some people have developed in areas of understanding and remained ignorant in others. It's the Believer who has developed in his or her understanding of the gifts yet has remained fleshly in other areas. This is where we super-spiritualize everything in the Kingdom through our thinking that God would only give gifts to the Saints who are near perfect. Not so. He has given His gifts to Believers who aren't ignorant of them and desire them (1 Corinthians 12:1, 12:31, and 14:1).

A gift from God is not attained through mental assent. Your mind will not figure some things out. I'm not saying you must lose your mind to operate in the gifts of the Spirit, but your mind certainly has to yield to the Spirit for you to function in the gifts. One of my first experiences with this was back in 1993 when I was an intern pastor. Ken Krivohlovek was teaching on the gifts of the Spirit and then he allowed us to practice. My spirit was excited, but my mind was questioning, "Is this really God? Do I have a prophetic word from God or is it just me?" My mind doubted, but the Spirit inside of me was bubbling with excitement. I decided to speak out what I was hearing inside of me.

Ken said to me in front of others, "It sounds like you have done this before." I think that was my first public prophetic message, but I had been making prophetic declarations in private. When you say "Yes" to the Spirit of God, your mind is yielding to the Spirit. We have the choice to remain in our own thinking or yield to the flow and understanding of the Holy Spirit. That day marked a change in my life. No longer were fear, intimidation, and my limited understanding in control, but the Spirit inside of me was allowed to speak and give life to others. I yielded to the Holy Spirit and decided to not listen to my head.

Sometimes The Holy Spirit will give you information about a person. What He impresses upon your heart to say, may seem ridiculous. My wife Christi was ministering to women in Watertown, South Dakota, when she heard, "Tell this woman in front of you I want to jitterbug with her." Christi paused and thought, "That's weird, what should I say?" Christi decided to ask the woman, "Do you know what the jitterbug is?" The woman chuckled and said, "Yes." Christi proceeded, "I know this may sound strange to you, but I heard the Lord tell me to tell you that He wants to jitterbug with you." Her friends began to laugh as she was instantly touched by the Power of God. She began to weep and laugh as she was overwhelmed by His Presence.

After the meeting Christi and I had lunch with the pastors of the church at a Chinese restaurant. As we were sitting there, the lady and her friends who were at the meeting came into the restaurant full of joy and excitement. What we found out was powerful. The lady Christi had spoken over informed us that the word Christi had given her was amazing. She informed us that she had been in a contest for one year traveling the nation. Do you know what that contest was? You guessed it. A jitterbug contest. Too funny! You see, this woman was so touched because she realized how real God was through this word. She discovered, possibly for the first time, how intimate God wants to be with her. She had never been in a meeting like that and was a bit scared because she didn't quite understand. But afterwards she had no doubts because she encountered God. What a God we serve!

Several years ago I went to an event called a Prophetic Round Table. I wasn't sure what to expect, but I went with a hunger to hear from God. People gathered together in Mandan, North Dakota, from various locations throughout North Dakota. We were asked to get into a group of six to eight, pray for one another, and share a word you may be getting for someone. People were sharing great words, and I stood there in great anticipation for a word from God.

Finally it was my time to receive a word. A red-headed girl from West Fargo looked at me and said, "I have a word for you: piano." That's about all she said, and my mind was speaking to me, "Where is this going? Piano. Is that it? I came to this event for this?" She proceeded, "Do you play piano?" I said, "I played piano for three years. My first two years I received a superior at my recital and the third year an excellent." She said, "Okay, that's all I get." My mind was reeling. "That was strange. Is there anything to this? Hmm." A key to receiving a word is not being quick to dismiss it.

After the breakout session was over, I went to a mentor of mine, Pastor Jim Hessler, and told him of the word I just heard. He chuckled and asked me, "Have you ever played piano?" My response was the same as before, "I played piano for three years. My first two years I received a superior at my recital, and the third year an excellent." Pastor Jim asked, "How many years have you been in your current traveling ministry?" I said, "We have almost completed two years and now are going into our third year." He responded, "Well, I believe the Lord is saying your first two years have been superior, don't blow it your third." Wow! That actually made sense. Sometimes we become comfortable to the point of not pushing ourselves to go the extra mile.

The story doesn't end just yet. When I arrived home after the event, I walked into our house, and my wife hugged me and said shortly after my arrival, "Your mom called and was wanting to know if we wanted the piano you played on when you were younger." Weird? Coincidence? Or God? I choose God! Christi wasn't at the event, nor was my mother. I had not told Christi about the word until after she spoke to me about my mom calling and asking about the piano. That sealed something in me that day. I chose to press in and position myself for a great third year on the road. God is good! He knows us, prepares us, and He loves us to have victory in all situations.

Truth

Gifts of The Spirit

"For I long to see you, that I may impart to you some spiritual gift to strengthen you."

(Romans 1:11)

"Now concerning spiritual gifts, brothers, I do not want you to be uninformed."

(1 Corinthians 12:1)

"To each is given the manifestation of the Spirit for the common good. For to one is given through the Spirit the utterance of wisdom, and to another the utterance of knowledge according to the same Spirit, to another faith by the same Spirit, to another gifts of healing by the one Spirit, to another the working of miracles, to another prophecy, to another the ability to distinguish between spirits, to another various kinds of tongues, to another the interpretation of tongues. All these are empowered by one and the same Spirit, who apportions to each one individually as he wills."

(1 Corinthians 12:7-11)

"Pursue love, and earnestly desire the spiritual gifts, especially that you may prophesy."

(1 Corinthians 14:1)

"For this reason I remind you to fan into flame the gift of God, which is in you through the laying on of my hands, for God gave us a spirit not of fear but of power and love and self-control."

(2 Timothy 1:6-7)

Think about it...

1. Are the gifts of The Holy Spirit important? Why?

2. Why doesn't God want us ignorant of spiritual gifts?

3. Is it O.K. to desire spiritual gifts? Why?

4. Who does God give spiritual gifts to?

5. Do you desire spiritual gifts? Why or why not?

9
Love Gifts from God

"And if I have prophetic powers, and understand all mysteries and all knowledge, and if I have all faith, so as to remove mountains, but have not love, I am nothing"

(1 Corinthians 13:2).

"I believe that one of the biggest reasons that the body of Christ hasn't made a greater impact on our generation today is because of our failure to operate in the gifts of the Holy Spirit."

—Andrew Womack

HAVE YOU EVER wondered why Paul wrote about the gifts of the Holy Spirit recorded in 1 Corinthians 12 and 14 and sandwiched in the middle is chapter 13, which is known as the "love chapter"? Paul starts writing about the gifts, then shifts to love, and then back to the gifts. I see a valuable purpose behind this message. The gifts are powerful, but essentially, these are the love gifts of the Holy Spirit.

The gifts operate through faith (1 Corinthians 12:6), and faith works through love (Galatians 5:6). Without love, faith and the gifts of the Holy Spirit don't have the eternal effect God intended for them to have.

The love of God reaches people in every season of their life. During the good seasons and the tough seasons, God's expression of love is always being manifested in various ways. One way that God expresses His love to people is through the gifts of the Holy Spirit. This is why Paul emphatically writes, "I don't want you to be uninformed" and "earnestly desire the most helpful gifts" (1 Corinthians 12:1, 12:31). The Lord wants Believers to be equipped to minister the Love Gifts of the Holy Spirit to their generation. If we really love people like we say we do, wouldn't we find God's way to express that love? Your emotions and your mind aren't enough to reach this generation for Christ, you need His grace; you need His gifts!

When I was struggling with depression in college, I was seeking and desperately searching for answers. I was oppressed with thoughts of suicide and without a solution as to why these thoughts were plaguing my mind. One Wednesday night at a Bible study and prayer meeting, a gentleman by the name of Larry stood up and testified about how God set him free from depression and thoughts of suicide. After the meeting that night, I bee-lined it over to Larry and told him about my struggles and how his testimony gave me hope. Friend, don't stop sharing your stories of victories. Someone needs to hear it!

Larry prayed for me that night in 1991. Larry not only prayed for me, he had a word of knowledge from the Holy Spirit, "You need to forgive." Larry proceeded to share with me who he felt I needed to forgive. The word of knowledge brought some clarification to me. After that encounter I went to the altar and began to pray and ask

God to forgive me for holding a grudge, and I chose once again to forgive and live. The word of knowledge was God's love compelling me to choose life and find healing and restoration through forgiveness.

The gifts of the Holy Spirit also bring confirmation to the will of God for your life. My sister, Kendra, was on a mission trip with us in 1998. Kendra was at a crossroads in her life. She had just received an invitation to be a pastor on staff somewhere in New Mexico. When Kendra told me about this offer, I didn't feel like it was the right thing for her to do at that time. I didn't tell her that. I just listened. Sandy, a participant on the mission trip, came to me and told me she had a word for my sister. Sandy was just learning about the gifts and how they operate. She was a little apprehensive in giving the word but felt strongly impressed to give it to Kendra.

I asked Sandy what she was hearing. Sandy said, "I hear Mexico, and Kendra is not supposed to go there right now." Wow! Sandy had been saved less than two years but was eagerly desiring the gifts of God. Because of this yearning, Sandy became a vessel through which the Lord could speak. I told Sandy, "I think you better share that with my sister." No brainer, right? Sandy shared, and my sister received the message which kept her on the right track.

God loved us so much he sent His Son Jesus, and Jesus loved us so much He sent the Holy Spirit to minister life to us and through us (John 3:16 and 16:7). The gifts of the Holy Spirit aren't meant for just a few superstars or super spiritual people; they are God's gifts to all who earnestly desire them and want to follow the way of love. "Follow the way of love and eagerly desire gifts of the Spirit, especially prophecy." (1 Corinthians 14:1, NIV). It's simple: ask and you shall receive!

Truth

Love One Another

"A new commandment I give to you, that you love one another: just as I have loved you, you also are to love one another. By this all people will know that you are my disciples, if you have love for one another."

(John 13:34-35)

"This is my commandment, that you love one another as I have loved you."

(John 15:12)

"Love one another with brotherly affection. Outdo one another in showing honor."

(Romans 12:10)

"Let all that you do be done in love."

(1 Corinthians 16:14)

"Let brotherly love continue."

(Hebrews 13:1)

"By this we know love, that he laid down his life for us, and we ought to lay down our lives for the brothers."

(1 John 3:16)

"Beloved, let us love one another, for love is from God, and whoever loves has been born of God and knows God. Anyone who does not love does not know God, because God is love."

(1 John 4:7-8)

Think about it...

1. What are the gifts of The Holy Spirit? List them.

2. How do they operate or function?

3. Who can minister with the gifts of The Holy Spirit?

4. Have you ministered with the gifts of The Holy Spirit? What was your experience? How did it help other people?

10
A Shout out for the Local Church

"And let us consider how to stir up one another to love and good works, not neglecting to meet together, as is the habit of some, but encouraging one another, and all the more as you see the Day drawing near"

(Hebrews 10:24–25).

"I was glad when they said to me, 'Let us go to the house of the LORD!'"

(Psalm 122:1).

I'M A STRONG proponent for the local church. I discovered what life was like without a local church for a very short season of my life. I was a freshman in college, wanting to spread my wings and discover "the world" without the church and the accountability of brothers and sisters in Christ. How did that work for me? Glad you asked. I made some of the poorest decisions I have ever made in my life. I am grateful for a loving and forgiving God.

When I got plugged back into a church that preached the Gospel and loved people, I began to thrive. After my experience of being delivered from oppression, depression, and the horrible tormenting thoughts of suicide, I was glad to be part of a local church that walked with me during the healing process. I am eternally grateful for pastors like Dan Rothwell, who allowed the Holy Spirit to move mightily amongst people in our weekly gatherings. If Pastor Dan had been fearful of the manifest presence of God, who knows what my life would look like today? Thank you, sir!

A strong and healthy local church has several attributes that provide for a culture in which Christians may grow. My experiences at First Assembly in Fargo were monumental to me. The following is a short list of what I learned after being plugged into the local church in Fargo.

1) **Church should be a safe place.** I was able to grow and be healed because I found people I could trust and confide in. Pastor Brad Lewis was our college Pastor. Brad wasn't condemning but loving. Brad didn't pretend to understand, but he chose to love. Trust me, I was a mess and didn't understand myself 90 percent of the time. Thank you, Brad, for the wise counsel and the grace to see beyond the pain.

Scott Stensgard was another pastor on staff at the church. Scott was a close friend. I was not enjoyable to be around for several months when I went through the valley. I dripped with oppression and, honestly, self pity. I will never forget the day Scott pulled me out of my apartment to get some fresh air. What was Scott doing? He was investing his time into someone who couldn't give much back. The local church should be a safe place where people see the destiny of a person beyond the dread.

2) **Church should be a place of sharpening.** You have probably read the Scripture, "As iron sharpens iron, so one person sharpens another" (Proverbs 27:17). I experienced this with a close friend in college, Joel Nix. Joel and I sharpened one another. Both of us were seeking Jesus and attempting to work out our salvation with fear and much trembling. Honestly, we didn't always agree on everything. We had heartfelt and difficult conversations at times. Those conversations were used to shape our lives like a file used to shape its object. Joel remains a close friend to this day.

3) **God's Word should be taught at Church.** I hated missing Sunday meetings at our church because of the teaching ministry of Dan Rothwell. Pastor Dan taught the Word of God in such a way that made it applicable throughout the week. Whether he had three points or thirteen, God's Word was honored and taught with much preparation by Pastor Dan. Most good meals take time.

Pastor Dan taught on stewardship every February. I can still remember a point he made: "Deny the lesser for the greater." That truth has helped me many of time walking through a mall.

4) **Church should be a place for His Presence.** When we gather together on Sunday mornings, God's manifest Presence is our friend, not foe. The praise and worship of the people rise and He descends. "Yet you are holy, enthroned on the praises of Israel" (Psalm 22:3). The Hebrew word for enthroned is "yashab," which means to dwell, remain, sit, or abide. When a local church ascends with the Praises of God, He sits in our presence and desires to be a large part of our meeting.

My experience with praise and worship at First Assembly changed my life. For the first time in my church experience, I was encouraged to express myself fully in praise. People were dancing, shouting, and clapping. I didn't see anyone hanging from the chandeliers, but I'm sure they would have if the ceiling hadn't been 50 feet high (joke). Because the culture of that church allowed for expression, I felt the liberty to dance, shout, and clap too. We don't praise God for our benefit, but the truth is, when we choose to praise and worship with abandonment, we receive the blessing of experiencing His Presence at a whole new level.

Our praise and worship leader in Fargo was Pastor Bruce Larson. He led with excellence, passion, and instruction. It's important to have this mix. Some people think they don't have to be prepared to lead others in praise and worship. Not so. Praise and worship is not a time slot to fill for Sundays or whenever your church meets; it's a vital part of what we do to engage the King of Glory.

Ruth Heflin ministered for nearly forty years with a love for Israel, evangelism, discipleship, and The Glory of God. Ruth said something that has stuck with me for almost twenty years now, "Praise until the Spirit of Worship comes, Worship until the Glory comes, then stand in His Glory." Pastor Bruce did this week after week.

Sometimes we sing our songs, God's Presence shows up, and then—bam—we shift the service abruptly without dwelling in His manifest Presence. It's like we are afraid of what might happen next. Don't be afraid. Dwell! He will do mighty things in our midst. You better watch out; I'm about ready to preach here.

What is our goal on Sunday mornings? At Freedom Church we desire to be great hosts to everyone who comes on Sunday morning and superb hosts to the King of kings and Lord of lords! Why ask

Him to come and then not give Him a chance to move and minister amongst the people? Yes, I am saying we can prohibit the King from having reign in our meetings. He will never force us to yield; He gives us that choice. I'm not saying He will not attempt to get our attention abruptly like He did with the Apostle Paul. He will demonstrate His power to this generation! I am saying He likes to work with His people and not strive with us.

May we never become like the church of Laodicea where Jesus stood outside the door knocking: "Behold, I stand at the door and knock. If anyone hears my voice and opens the door, I will come in to him and eat with him, and he with me" (Revelation 3:20). We apply that Scripture to sinners. That message was to the people of God in Laodicea and applies to Believers today! Notice Jesus didn't say, "I stand at the door, you aren't answering, so I'm about to bust this door down!" No. It's more like an invitation to churches everywhere to abide and sit with Jesus for the sake of building a strong, life-giving relationship.

Is Jesus still knocking at our door? I think the goal for us is to continually have Him in our house so He doesn't have to keep knocking.

I am eternally grateful for my experience at First Assembly in Fargo—before and after my deliverance experience. When you have a safe place amongst the community of Believers to sharpen yourself, receive counsel from the Word of God, and experience His Manifest Presence, the process of healing and restoration becomes much more accessible.

Truth

The Church

"And I tell you, you are Peter, and on this rock I will build my church, and the gates of hell shall not prevail against it."

(Matthew 16:18)

"And they devoted themselves to the apostles' teaching and the fellowship, to the breaking of bread and the prayers. And awe came upon every soul, and many wonders and signs were being done through the apostles. And all who believed were together and had all things in common. And they were selling their possessions and belongings and distributing the proceeds to all, as any had need. And day by day, attending the temple together and breaking bread in their homes, they received their food with glad and generous hearts, praising God and having favor with all the people. And the Lord added to their number day by day those who were being saved."

(Acts 2:42-47)

"So we, though many, are one body in Christ, and individually members one of another."

(Romans 12:5)

"So then you are no longer strangers and aliens, but you are fellow citizens with the saints and members of the household of God, built on the foundation of the apostles and prophets, Christ Jesus himself being the cornerstone, in whom the whole structure, being joined together, grows into a holy temple in the Lord. In him you also are being built together into a dwelling place for God by the Spirit."

(Ephesians 2:19-22)

"He who descended is the one who also ascended far above all the heavens, that he might fill all things.) And he gave the apostles, the prophets, the evangelists, the shepherds and teachers, to equip the saints for the work of ministry, for building up the body of Christ, until we all attain to the unity of the faith and of the knowledge of the Son of God, to mature manhood, to the measure of the stature of the fullness of Christ, so that we may no longer be children, tossed to and fro by the waves and carried about by every wind of doctrine, by human cunning, by craftiness in deceitful schemes. Rather, speaking the truth in love, we are to grow up in every way into him who is the head, into Christ, from whom the whole body, joined and held together by every joint with which it is equipped, when each part is working properly, makes the body grow so that it builds itself up in love."

(Ephesians 4:10-16)

"And let us consider how to stir up one another to love and good works, not neglecting to meet together, as is the habit of some, but encouraging one another, and all the more as you see the Day drawing near."

(Hebrews 10:24-25)

Think about it...

1. Do you go to church? Why?

2. What has been your experience of church life?

3. List four attributes of a healthy church.

11
The Rising Tide of God's Leaders

"Have I not commanded you? Be strong and courageous. Do not be frightened, and do not be dismayed, for the Lord your God is with you wherever you go"

(Joshua 1:9).

"Young people need models, not critics."

—John Wooden

I SEE THE emergence of the greatest leaders this planet has ever seen at one moment in time. These mighty men and women of God are rising like the tide of an ocean coming to our shores. "When the tide is rising and the flow of the current is directed towards the shore, the tidal current is called the flood current (Jennifer Horton, *How Stuff Works*)." I believe a flood of young and old leaders are rising with a message of reconciliation and power.

We often hear about the young leaders who are rising, but what about the old leaders who still have gas in their tank? Leaders with an attitude like Caleb, who, at eighty-five years of age, said, "I am still as strong today as I was in the day that Moses sent me; my strength now is as my strength was then, for war and for going and coming. So now give me this hill country of which the LORD spoke on that day" (Joshua 14:11–12). Caleb knew the promise and contended in faith for it to manifest while he had breath on this Earth.

How many promises have been relinquished because we simply gave in to the lie that the fulfillment of our promise from God is for another generation? Not Caleb! He reminded Joshua of the promise spoken by Moses: "Surely the land on which your foot has trodden shall be an inheritance for you and your children forever, because you have wholly followed the LORD my God" (Joshua 14:9). Caleb believed God's promise through Moses and took hold of that which was promised to him. He did not relent. He was like a dog to a bone. He bit down, he bit hard, and he would not let go until he saw with his own eyes the promise fulfilled. "And now, behold, the LORD has kept me alive, just as He said, these forty-five years since the time that the LORD spoke this word to Moses, while Israel walked in the wilderness. And now, behold, I am this day eighty-five years old" (Joshua 14:10). Don't give up and don't listen to the doubts that assail you. The promise is coming!

Currently we have two people in our church who are in their eighties. Both are actively praying and serving at the church in ways they are able to serve. Both are givers and not takers. They are from a golden generation of hard workers who have seen tough days but have watched the Mighty Hand of God move in their lives. They serve as encouragers and intercessors. Their wives have passed on to Heaven while they continue to fight the good fight of faith here on Earth. Just recently they stood on our church land and loudly spoke out with a group of people, "Take the Mountain!" They were declaring, "We want to see this building built on this land before we die!" So be it, Jesus. So be it!

A lot has been said about the younger generation—some good and plenty of bad. The younger generation is simply a reflection of the one previous to them, good and bad. I'm not going to give you my rating of the younger generation; rather, I am going to prophesy what I see and what I hear. God's view is always more complete even though we see in part.

I see the rising tide of some the greatest leaders the planet has ever experienced. Though tides of evil blow to our shores, God is raising a standard amongst young leaders that is out of this world. I see the face of a lion arising in our midst. This lion will roar through these young leaders. This lion is Jesus, the Christ inside of them displaying His might and courage. These young leaders will demonstrate the courage that is necessary to overcome in a world that is pressing to overcome them.

Their cry is "Help me! I need the older generation to cheer me on, not condemn me. I need you to encourage and guide me, not compete against me. I'm here to stay, so father and mother me to greatness." Paul nailed it when he wrote, "For though you have countless guides in Christ, you do not have many fathers. For I became your father in Christ Jesus through the gospel" (1 Corinthians 4:15). Many instructors, few fathers.

A father loves his children and wants the best for them. A father will encourage, advise, and bring correction when necessary. A father will lay down his life and rights to see the son or daughter rise to his or her potential. A father will also take responsibility to impart what he knows to the next generation. A father is a covering, a safe place for the young to develop.

An instructor is necessary, but may not be as deeply invested into the process of development as a father is. Please don't misinterpret what I'm saying. Instructors can be fathers or mothers to the next generation. It's all about the perspective and heart posture towards these sons and daughters.

Tony Cooke gives a descriptive explanation on his website (www.tonycooke.org) of a Spiritual Father through traits he observed in the life of the Apostle Paul. The following ten traits are observed by Tony:

1. He did not flatter them (1 Thessalonians 2:5). He wasn't buttering them up just so they'd like him or so he could get something out of them.
2. He was not covetous toward them (1 Thessalonians 2:5). He didn't see having a relationship with them as a means of getting their goods.
3. He did not seek glory of men; he wasn't seeking to be exalted (1 Thessalonians 2:6). This wasn't about Paul gathering sons around him to feed his own ego.
4. He was not demanding of them. He wasn't controlling, manipulative, or dictatorial (1 Thessalonians 2:6).
5. He exhibited a heartfelt, compassionate concern for their well-being.
    a. He was gentle toward them (1 Thessalonians 2:7).
    b. He cherished them (1 Thessalonians 2:7).
    c. He longed for them affectionately (1 Thessalonians 2:8).
    d. He not only gave them the gospel, but he gave his own life to them (1 Thessalonians 2:8).
    e. They were dear to him (1 Thessalonians 2:8).
    f. He exhorted, comforted, and charged every one of them, as a father does his children (1 Thessalonians 2:11).

6. His energies and efforts went toward their spiritual development (Galatians 4:19).
7. He was not interested in shaming them but did feel obligated to warn them. He wasn't putting them on a guilt trip or making them feel intimidated (1 Corinthians 4:14).
8. He was different than a mere teacher; he wasn't just passing information on to them, but he had "begotten them" through the Gospel and was setting an example they could follow in their spiritual development (1 Corinthians 4:15–16).
9. He wasn't seeking what was theirs (their money), but he was seeking *them* (2 Corinthians 12:14).
10. He was willing to spend and be spent for them; in other words, he was willing to live and give sacrificially for them—for their advancement and their development (2 Corinthians 12:15).

The question yet remains, "Where are the spiritual fathers?" The founder and bishop of Grace Christian Fellowship International Churches, Dave Chikosi, says some strong words: "We need fathers in the church. Unfortunately we have a bunch of babysitters and hirelings pretending to be fathering our spiritual sons and daughters. The result is that the church has become an orphanage rather than a family." Strong words—but are they true? Have we empowered our leaders to become spiritual fathers, or have we trained them to be leaders who don't really lead but follow the dictates of the governing board of our churches?

In my observation of church leadership for the past thirty years, I have seen both a picture of spiritual fathers leading as well as leaders who have attempted to rise but never attain that place in the people's hearts. Respect is earned; it doesn't come with a title or even a grandiose vision. I wish I would have known that when my wife and I planted Freedom Worship Center in 2006. I figured I had proven myself in ministry because I completed six years of ministry as a youth pastor and six years traveling and preaching in over forty-five different churches.

What I didn't realize was, I may have ministered for twelve years, but not to the people of Aberdeen, SD. Christi and I were excited and passionate about our God-given vision, but passion and excitement doesn't automatically give you influence nor does it earn respect from the people you are leading. Respect comes through time, displaying integrity, courage, perseverance, and loyalty to the call of God on your life. I expected to blow in with the wind and have overnight success because I traveled six years and saw a measure of success as a youth pastor. Yes, this is a good time to laugh.

The old saying is true, "People don't care how much you know until they know how much you care." I thought I could pull out my trophies and victorious stories of my past to wow everyone, but the truth is I had to prove myself again. Somehow I thought that season of my life was over (laugh again). I discovered that season never ends! If you are growing in your leadership, it will expand into new areas, and the proving starts all over.

I claim to be no expert in leadership or church development, so please understand this before you continue to read the following remarks from my own observation. Churches rise and fall upon leadership. When a leader or pastor comes to a local church and shares his or her vision with great passion, then leaves that church after two years because "The Lord is leading me in another direction," that church will develop trust issues with leadership. If the cycle continues, that local church will begin to form walls of steel five feet thick.

We all have heard or observed churches with people who have control issues. Leaders/pastors quickly point out these people as "control freaks," and they have to lose control so the leader can lead. We sometimes fail to ask the right questions, such as "Why do these people have issues in the first place?" If a local church has pastors coming and going every two to four years, is it any wonder why these local churches have a difficult time relinquishing control yet to another grandiose vision? The people have lost trust in leadership and that trust must be restored somehow. How is the vicious cycle going to stop?

It begins with the leader/pastor. The new pastor must commit in his or her heart that he or she is in this for the long haul. Not an easy commitment to make, but a necessary one. Healing will never manifest in that broken local church until the leader decides to persevere through the painful times. That five-foot-thick steel wall cannot be penetrated in a few short years. Trust is restored when the leader remains passionate about the people of his or her community becoming Disciples of Jesus Christ.

Secondly, a process of forgiveness must begin in the hearts of the local church. They cannot hang onto the baggage of yesterday. A deep sense of disappointment enters the hearts of the local church people because they let down their walls only to see yet another pastor leave because "God told them to." The church begins to form a mentality of an orphan rather than sons or daughters. Abandonment and disappointment are the roots, and the fruit is distrust, critical spirits, gossip, and control.

The hearts of people are difficult to lead when offended. The wise man wrote, "An offended friend is harder to win back than a fortified city. Arguments separate friends like a gate locked with bars" (Proverbs 18:19, NLT). The people in the local church may not be directly offended at you, but they are offended at your position, and the ones who filled that position before you. When walking through this struggle and pain with people, it's important to remind yourself as the leader to not take offense yourself. Constant reminders of "hurting people hurt people" and "forgive and live" are necessary in order to not become a casualty of war. This truly is a spiritual battle that can only be won with spiritual weapons. "For the weapons of our warfare are not of the flesh but have divine power to destroy strongholds" (2 Corinthians 10:4). Forgiveness is a powerful weapon that defeats the powers of darkness.

Jesus said, "It is impossible that no offenses should come" (Luke 17:1, KJV). You will be tempted not to forgive the people who are hurtful. When you find yourself defensive and retaliating in any way with words or actions, watch out! You are being driven by the flesh rather than being led by the Spirit. The flesh never produces fruit that will last nor will it profit you in any way. Choosing to forgive and release your offender is your only choice if you are going to remain the victorious leader that God has called you to be in this local church. It doesn't matter if they deserve to be forgiven; none of us deserve to be forgiven. The issue is keeping our hearts guarded and remaining unoffended so we can reach the people God has called and anointed us to reach.

We are called to be "wise as serpents and innocent as doves" (Matthew 10:16). If our enemy can outwit us through offenses, we lose the battle of winning back the hearts of the people we are called to lead. Father God never said this would be easy, but He did say, "Many are the afflictions of the righteous, but the Lord delivers him out of them all" (Psalm 34:19). The wounds of others sometimes become a season of affliction for us as leaders. Don't let the wounds of others infect you; let them shape you. Remember, God delivers you out of them all!

Paul wrote, "For this light momentary affliction is preparing for us an eternal weight of glory beyond all comparison, as we look not to the things that are seen but to the things that are unseen. For the things that are seen are transient, but the things that are unseen are eternal" (2 Corinthians 4:17–18). It's important we see in the Spirit and not merely be overwhelmed by our present struggle. The present struggle is a season, but the lessons imparted to you during the struggle are eternal. Remember, churches rise and fall upon great leadership. God is forming you to be a leader of tens, twenties, hundreds and/or thousands.

Truth

Kingdom Leadership

"Have I not commanded you? Be strong and courageous. Do not be frightened, and do not be dismayed, for the Lord your God is with you wherever you go."

(Joshua 1:9)

"With upright heart he shepherded them and guided them with his skillful hand."

(Psalm 78:72)

"And Jesus called them to him and said to them, 'You know that those who are considered rulers of the Gentiles lord it over them, and their great ones exercise authority over them. But it shall not be so among you. But whoever would be great among you must be your servant, and whoever would be first among you must be slave of all. For even the Son of Man came not to be served but to serve, and to give his life as a ransom for many.'"

(Mark 10:42-45)

"Do nothing from selfish ambition or conceit, but in humility count others more significant than yourselves."

(Philippians 2:3)

"Not looking each of you to his own things, but each of you also to the things of others."

(Philippians 2:4)

"Remember your leaders, those who spoke to you the word of God. Consider the outcome of their way of life, and imitate their faith."

(Hebrews 13:7)

"Let no one despise you for your youth, but set the believers an example in speech, in conduct, in love, in faith, in purity."

(1 Timothy 4:12)

"Be diligent to present yourself approved to God as a workman who does not need to be ashamed, accurately handling the word of truth."

(2 Timothy 2:15)

Think about it...

1. Do you believe God has a purpose and plan for your life? Why?

2. Can you see what His purpose is for you?

3. What is the greatest fear of your future?

4. What do you see for the younger generation?

5. What is a spiritual father or mother? Do you have one?

6. Have you ever been offended? How did that offense affect you?

7. How can you rid yourself of offenses and harboring bitterness?

8. When do you know you have really forgiven someone from your heart?

12
Don't Give Up!

"And let us not grow weary of doing good, for in due season we will reap, if we do not give up"

(Galatians 6:9).

"You can enjoy the luxury of wanting to quit if you know you're not going to quit."

—Tommy Barnett

A THOUSAND TIMES I have wanted to quit. It's that moment in your life when the pain of the present outweighs the glory of your future. You know that saying: "I just quit! I can't handle this anymore!" What does that mean? To some it's a cry for help. To others it's a way of releasing pain in order to embrace the promise, and sadly for some, they do quit.

I am grateful for my dad who has been a great example of one who never quits. I remember my dad being depressed. It lasted about two days. He was struggling with a major decision pertaining to his career and wasn't able to see clearly what decision he should make. I remember my dad sitting on a chair wrapped in a comforter without much to say and very little ambition. Fortunately, he got up the next day and faced life head on by making a decision. Quit was not in my dad's vocabulary and to this day, at the age of seventy-five, he doesn't know the word nor does he embrace it.

Growing up, I learned not to quit. Did I want to quit? Absolutely! Football was a sport I loved to play. I was big for my age in elementary and middle school, so I had an advantage over the smaller boys. My talent matched my size, so my vision of being a future star athlete was blazing within me. Little did I know that I would stop growing, and everyone's size and talent would catch up to me eventually.

By the time I was a senior in high school, I was 185 pounds and just under 5 foot, 10 inches. My height had not increased since the ninth grade. I had to fight hard to be a starter for the Aberdeen Central Golden Eagles. I lifted weights and ran with some of the teammates during the summer months to get an edge.

My football season started with great promise. I made the starting line up as one of the running backs and sole punt returner. I was in! As one of the running backs, I naturally thought I would be running with the ball. Well, I did very little running and mostly blocking. The one time I did run with the ball, I swept around the end and gained twenty-five yards for our team. I was excited! The coach was mad. He was mad because I ran out of bounce rather than putting my head down and plowing over my defender. Sorry, coach.

My senior year was plagued with that feeling of never being able to satisfy my coach. Please don't get me wrong; my coach was great. He went to the next level of coaching after my senior year—great guy. Though he was a great guy and completely qualified, my perception was, "I can never do enough to please this guy." Who said sports is not mental and emotional? We think of the physicality it takes to be a great athlete, but it requires so much more. Mental and emotional toughness is required.

My coach was on my case a lot my senior year. He must have seen greatness in me and was attempting to pull it out of me. But the more he yelled at me, the more angry and withdrawn I became. I remember him yelling while we were conditioning, "Becker, if you don't finish first the whole team will run more!" No pressure, right? I think the team was smart enough to appear like they were running their fastest but applying the brakes a little, you know what I mean?

I didn't mind the yelling as long as I was playing, but that came to an abrupt end after the fourth or fifth game of the season. I began to watch the games from the sidelines—great time (sarcasm). If you're going to bench someone in the middle of the year, at least give them an explanation and stop yelling at them during practices (I feel much better after saying that, lol!). I will never forget the practice we had prior to a big game towards the end of the year. Our coach decided to concoct a new play that included me running the ball. The play was a trick play that required a lineman to pull and the timing between me, the quarterback, and the lineman to be impeccable.

After running the play about twenty-five times with the coach "in my grill" the entire time, I had enough. I mean, I had enough! It was the first and last time in my entire life that I looked at the coach and yelled and swore at him. The entire team and assistant coaches got real quiet. The only thing that my head coach said was, "Becker, sit down." I don't think we ever ran that play in a game. In fact, the only time I got on the playing field was for pre-game warm ups, punt returning, and running across the field after the game was over.

Did I want to quit football my senior year? You bet I did! When you don't feel like you're making much of a contribution to your fellow teammates, you begin to feel the deep-seated pain of isolation and rejection. Some personalities would just "blow it off" and make the best of a bad situation. Not me. I took it very personally, yet I didn't quit. I chose to finish the year out with my friends.

We went into the playoffs that year, got to the second round, and were defeated 7–0. The coach gave me the instructions to not call for a fair catch no matter what. The first and only punt I returned that game was high in the air, and my blocker decided to move out of the way from the 230-pound defender who was running with a head full of steam. As soon as I touched the ball I was laying on the ground thinking, "Wow, what just happened?" My dad said he could hear the hit from the bleachers. I wasn't knocked out, I don't think. Somehow I managed not to drop the ball.

After that game my coach who had consistently yelled at me, announced me the MVP of the game. For years, whenever I saw that plaque, I thought to myself, "He just gave that MVP of the game plaque to me because he felt bad for yelling at me the entire year." Today I know that plaque was a reward for not quitting. God rewards those for diligently seeking Him (Hebrews 11:6). He also emphatically commands us,

> "Do not, therefore, fling away your fearless confidence, for it carries a great and glorious compensation of reward. For you have need of steadfast patience and endurance, so that you may perform and fully accomplish the will of God, and thus receive and carry away [and enjoy to the full] what is promised."
>
> (Hebrews 10:35–36, AMP)"

Did you get that? Don't fling away your trust! Don't give up! Persevere and fulfill the will of God for your life. Your choices not only impact you but they affect your present and future teammates in life. Had I quit my senior year of football, I would have started a lifestyle of quitting before I could receive my reward. Our reward in the Kingdom is to hear our Father say on that day in Heaven, "This is My beloved Son, in Whom I am well pleased! You finished the race, you never quit! Enter into My rest." Thanks, Dad, for not quitting. You touched me and the generations to come!

Truth

Hope & Courage

"Have I not commanded you? Be strong and courageous. Do not be frightened, and do not be dismayed, for the Lord your God is with you wherever you go."

(Joshua 1:9)

"But you, take courage! Do not let your hands be weak, for your work shall be rewarded."

(2 Chronicles 15:7)

"It is the Lord who goes before you. He will be with you; he will not leave you or forsake you. Do not fear or be dismayed."

(Deuteronomy 31:8)

"But they who wait for the LORD shall renew their strength; they shall mount up with wings like eagles; they shall run and not be weary; they shall walk and not faint."

(Isaiah 40:31)

"When you pass through the waters, I will be with you; and through the rivers, they shall not overwhelm you; when you walk through fire you shall not be burned, and the flame shall not consume you."

(Isaiah 43:2)

"For I know the plans I have for you, declares the Lord, plans for welfare and not for evil, to give you a future and a hope."

(Jeremiah 29:11)

"May the God of hope fill you with all joy and peace in believing, so that by the power of the Holy Spirit you may abound in hope."

(Romans 15:13)

"But thanks be to God, who gives us the victory through our Lord Jesus Christ. Therefore, my beloved brothers, be steadfast, immovable, always abounding in the work of the Lord, knowing that in the Lord your labor is not in vain."

(1 Corinthians 15:57)

"And let us not grow weary of doing good, for in due season we will reap, if we do not give up."

(Galatians 6:9)

"And I am sure of this, that he who began a good work in you will bring it to completion at the day of Jesus Christ."

(Philippians 1:6)

"Therefore encourage one another and build one another up, just as you are doing."

(1 Thessalonians 5:11)

Think about it...

1. Why is it important for you, not to quit?

2. Why do so many people give up? How can you help them?

3. Can quitting become a life-long pattern? How do you break that pattern?

4. What is your plan to finish strong?

13
Who's Chasing Who?

"I was FOUND by those who did NOT seek me; I revealed myself to those who did not ask for me"

(Romans 10:20).

"For thus says the Lord God: Behold, I Myself will search for My sheep and seek them out"

(Ezekiel 34:11).

FOR TWENTY-PLUS YEARS, I have preached the message of hungering after God and going after Him with your whole heart. "You will seek me and find me, when you seek me with all your heart" (Jeremiah 29:13). I will continue to preach this message but along with it preach, "God is chasing after you!" God spoke to Moses: "for you shall worship no other god, for the LORD, whose name is Jealous, is a jealous God" (Exodus 34:14). The jealousy of God is about His intense love for people and His desire to become your intimate friend.

When I was nine years old, my cousin Tory told me, "You are going to hell, and so is your whole family." Quite bold! Probably not the best way to lead others to Christ. Tory got saved after his sister, father, and mother had a radical conversion to Christ. Their family began to pray for our family to surrender to the Lordship of Jesus. Tory's heart wasn't bad; he was scared for us, and rightfully so.

Though Tory's approach wasn't appreciated at the time, it startled me and caused me to cry and approach my parents, who were not saved at the time. Tory's bold statement made an impact in my life. Thirty-eight years later, I still remember. How does God get our attention? How does He chase after us? Sometimes it begins with a bold statement, but often it begins with a question.

When God asks us a question, it's not because He doesn't know the answer. It's asked because *we* don't know the answer. Questions from God are invitations from Him to draw closer and become a student of His ways. The first recorded question from God to His people was, "Where are you?" (Genesis 3:9). Adam and Eve had sinned through a direct disobedient act against God's Word. After they sinned, shame, guilt, and fear drove them to attempt to hide from God.

I have often thought about this interaction between God and Adam and Eve in this story. At that point, God could have left them in a state of confusion. He could have said, "I told you so; now you are on your own." He could have turned His back on humanity at that point and been disgusted with the lack of respect and holiness. But God chose to approach them and chase after them. How does He do it? He reengages them through a question, "Where are you?" Was this for His sake or Adam and Eve's? Obviously not His.

He reengages them with a question, and the question brings them back into relationship with Him. We know their sinful act had negative repercussions, and I certainly don't want to dismiss that. However, God had a plan that He put into action immediately: "And I will put enmity between you and the woman, and between your offspring and hers; he will crush your head, and you will strike his heel" (Genesis 3:15). This is a prophetic proclamation of the Messiah crushing the head of Satan. The *Jamieson-Fausset-Brown Bible Commentary* says, "The serpent's poison is lodged in its head; and a bruise on that part is fatal." The fatal blow to Satan was at the Cross and the resurrection of Jesus Christ.

What was God saying? What was He doing? This Divine interaction with His creation in the Garden was disturbed by the devil, and God was going to restore that fellowship with man through His perfect sacrifice, His Son Jesus. Why did God create us with an option of whom we would serve? Why didn't He just create this Earth without the presence of evil and keep us in this "little bubble" of protection from all temptation? I believe He is looking for volunteer lovers rather than rigid robotic humanoids that don't have a choice. Guess what? We don't *have* to serve Him; we *get* to! God is looking for volunteer lovers who worship Him "in spirit and truth" (John 4:24).

Though man chose to do evil and not obey God in the garden, God chose to chase after people. I'm glad that He still chases after people! About a year after Tory made that bold statement, my parents surrendered their lives to Jesus. Tory's statement had to get my parents thinking and questioning their own relationship with Christ. Nine years after my family came to Christ, I was at a crossroads in my life during my first year of college. I turned my back on God's call for my life and surrendered my body to the flesh and the devil. Did God give up on me? No! He chased after me and began to approach me with questions.

Two guys from the dorm in which I was living asked me this bold question, "Drew, if you were to die today, do you know where you would go? Heaven or hell?" I also received a letter from a good friend back home encouraging me and challenging me to serve Jesus. Later that first year of college, a pastor from First Assembly in Fargo called me and met with me on campus. Pastor Curt proceeded to ask me questions. He said my mom was very worried about me and wanted him to talk to me immediately. What was happening? God was chasing after me. He never gives up. By April of my first year at college, I surrendered my heart to Christ in my dorm room on the twelfth floor of Neumaier Hall. What an awesome God we serve!

One of the most distinguishing differences between our God and others gods is He chases after us but doesn't kill us if we don't serve Him. He is patient with His people. "The Lord is not slow to fulfill his promise as some count slowness, but is patient toward you, not wishing that any should perish, but that all should reach repentance" (2 Peter 3:9). He doesn't want us to perish in our sin. He chases after us with His zeal to have a relationship with us. Nahum 1:7 declares, "The Lord is good." How true it is!

The beautiful truth is, God doesn't wait until we reach perfection until He chases us; He chases us in our sin: "But God shows his love for us in that while we were still sinners, Christ died for us" (Romans 5:8). God chose to love you knowing that you would sin and turn from Him, "for all have sinned and fall short of the glory of God" (Romans 3:23). We all have fallen short and sin leads to death, but God designed a plan of salvation from our sins, "For the wages of sin is death, but the free gift of God is eternal life in Christ Jesus our Lord. (Romans 6:23). The free gift of God. Wow! We don't have to earn our salvation by works. It's a free gift in Jesus Christ our Lord!

The only hope of salvation I can give you is Jesus Christ. Jesus said it himself, "I am the way, and the truth, and the life. No one comes to the Father except through me" (John 14:6). Giving the hope of salvation to someone without leading them to Christ is like giving a cup without water to someone dying from dehydration. The Apostle Peter boldly proclaimed, "And there is salvation in no one else, for there is no other name under heaven given among men by which we must be saved" (Acts 14:12). That name, my friend, is Jesus!

Who's chasing whom? God is chasing you with His zeal! He loves you with an everlasting, unconditional love. Twenty-eight years ago, I surrendered to God's passionate love for my soul. I stopped running and put up my white flag, and said, "Jesus, I need you! Please help me!" That life-changing, purpose-altering evening in 1988 rocked my world forever! Thank You, Jesus, for chasing me and saving me from the pit of despair and sin that controlled my life. Scripture tells us, "If you declare with your mouth, 'Jesus is Lord,' and believe in your heart that God raised him from the dead, you will be saved. For it is with your heart that you believe and are justified, and it is with your mouth that you profess your faith and are saved" (Romans 10:9–10). What are we saved from? From the condemnation of sin and an eternity in hell without Christ. Remember, He is not willing that anyone perish without His Son residing in their heart.

This journey with God begins with a simple prayer: "God, I need you. Today I surrender my will and my ways to You. Thank You for chasing me and never giving up on me. Thank You for sending Jesus to die for my sins. I believe today that Jesus is my personal savior from my sins. Jesus, please forgive me and cleanse me from the sins that are destroying my life. I ask you to be the King of my heart and lead my life from this moment on. Jesus, I believe you are Lord of all. Come and live in my heart. Amen." The journey begins by faith and continues in faith.

I want to pray a prayer over you that many of our Jewish friends have prayed for centuries:

The Lord bless you and keep you; the Lord make his face to shine upon you and be gracious to you; the Lord lift up his countenance upon you and give you peace.

(Numbers 6:24–26)

Truth

Salvation

"For whoever would save his life will lose it, but whoever loses his life for my sake and the gospel's will save it."

(Mark 8:35)

"For God so loved the world, that he gave his only Son, that whoever believes in him should not perish but have eternal life."

(John 3:16)

"For God did not send his Son into the world to condemn the world, but in order that the world might be saved through him."

(John 3:17)

"This Jesus is the stone that was rejected by you, the builders, which has become the cornerstone. And there is salvation in no one else, for there is no other name under heaven given among men by which we must be saved."

(Acts 4:11-12)

"Believe in the Lord Jesus, and you will be saved, you and your household."

(Acts 16:31)

"For all have sinned and fall short of the glory of God."

(Romans 3:23)

"But God shows his love for us in that while we were still sinners, Christ died for us."

(Romans 5:8)

"For the wages of sin is death, but the free gift of God is eternal life in Christ Jesus our Lord."

(Romans 6:23)

"Because, if you confess with your mouth that Jesus is Lord and believe in your heart that God raised him from the dead, you will be saved. For with the heart one believes and is justified, and with the mouth one confesses and is saved."

(Romans 10:9-10)

"Whoever has the Son has life; whoever does not have the Son of God does not have life."

(1 John 5:12)

Think about it...

1. What is the jealousy of God?

2. Who started the chase, God or man?

3. Who is the only hope for your salvation?

4. Are you saved? How do you know?

FREEDOM CHURCH

516 Production Street, Aberdeen, SD

www.time4freedom.org
605-725-0777

Sundays at 10:00AM

Our Mission
Freedom Church exists to encourage, equip, and enable people to walk in their God-given purpose through authentic, life-giving relationships and the dynamic presence of God.

Made in the USA
Lexington, KY
10 May 2017